reporter's
interview
with
Jesus

D0167017

Benton Rain Patterson

Tyndale House Publishers, Inc. | Wheaton, Illinois

Visit Tyndale's exciting Web site at http:\\www.tyndale.com

Designed by Justin Ahrens

Library of Congress Cataloging-in-Publication Data

Patterson, Benton Rain, 1929-
  A reporter's interview with Jesus / Benton Rain Patterson.
    p. cm.
  ISBN 0-8423-7171-0 (sc)
  1. Jesus Christ—Words. 2. Imaginary conversations. I. Title.
BT306.P355 2000
232.9′54—dc21   99-057370

Printed in the United States of America

05 04 03 02 01 00
8   7   6   5   4   3   2   1

Author's Preface

The reporter's words in this book are fictional. The words of Jesus are taken from the Gospels of Matthew, Mark, Luke, and John. A Scripture reference guide at the end of the book lists passages on which the words of Jesus are based.

B. R. P.

Meeting Him

Of course I had heard about him, but I had never met him or even heard him speak. So when I found out I was supposed to interview him, I had to hustle and learn as much as I could from people who had met or heard him. That turned out to be not so difficult. Once I began asking around, I discovered that a remarkable number of people had heard him. Most of those people, what's more, didn't mind saying what they thought about him.

Setting up the interview was a bigger problem. He was forever on the move, and it was hard to know, days in advance, where he was going to be and when he was going to be there. But after several unsuccessful attempts to make contact, I discovered that he had friends in Bethany, a community about two miles outside of Jerusalem, on the eastern side of the Mount of Olives, on the road to Jericho. I also learned that when he was in the vicinity of Jerusalem, he usually stayed with them. The friends were a widow as well as her unmarried younger sister and brother, who lived with her.

So I sent a letter to the widow, Martha, asking if she could put me in touch with him and telling her what I had in mind. I told her that I would like to spend several hours with him in a place where he would be relaxed and more or less undistracted by other people, and that my intention was to engage him in conversation, ask him questions about himself and what he was trying to do, faithfully record his answers, and finally put it all down so that audiences of readers could learn, through his words, what he was all about.

Martha wrote me back and said she would convey my request to him and that I would hear later either from her or from him or from one of his students. Within a couple of weeks I received another letter from her. He would do the interview, in just the way I had requested, and he would be staying at her house in Bethany, two weeks from then. I was invited to come and talk to him there.

By the time the interview date arrived, I had learned quite a bit about him, or at least what people had to say about him. And by then I was aware that I was really eager to do the interview. I was eager to meet him. If even half of what I was hearing about him was true, he was an absolutely extraordinary person. More than a few people I talked to told me that he had changed their lives. "He'll have an effect on you, in one way or another," one man told me. I found that prospect somewhat disturbing.

Martha's house was a three-story, flat-roofed stone building with several rooms and a small courtyard, on a narrow street, away from the highway. She had written me directions for finding it. It was a good thing I had requested a *private* meeting, because there was a small crowd in the courtyard when I got there. If I had had to compete with them for his attention, I don't think it would have been much of an interview.

With help from a couple of Jesus' students, I managed to find Martha. She was in the kitchen, dicing onions, presumably to go into one or more of the three pots that were on the cooking fire. A formidable-looking woman, she seemed to be holding her own despite having a swarm of guests descend on her all at once. "I can't stop now," she told me. "He's upstairs, probably talking with my sister. If so, you can tell her to come down here and give me a hand."

There were several people in the room with him. When I stopped and looked in, they greeted me. Apparently they knew why I was there because they excused themselves and left the room, leaving me alone with Jesus, who was sitting cross-legged on the floor, a reddish rug beneath him, his back against a wall. He was wearing an undyed robe and was barefooted.

I don't know exactly what I was expecting him to look like. But I had an image that had been formed in my mind by words that Isaiah the prophet had written more than seven centuries earlier. In preparation for the interview, I had re-read Isaiah's words, the ones that promised the coming of a messiah, since that was what a lot of people were saying Jesus was. He "grew up in the Lord's presence like a tender green shoot, sprouting from a root in dry and sterile ground," Isaiah wrote. "There was nothing beautiful or majestic about his appearance, nothing to attract us to him. He was despised and rejected—a man of sorrows, acquainted with bitterest grief."

Not a pretty picture. But Jesus, in the way he looked at least, didn't seem to fit that description. My impression was that he was a pleasant man, not especially nice-looking perhaps, but a man whose face was soft with sympathy and acceptance, a completely approachable person. He also seemed a man full of energy. His face, his eyes, his manner, his gestures all seemed to give off energy.

"Peace," he said and smiled, waving his hand toward me. "Please have a seat."

I smiled back. "Thank you. And peace be with you, too." I sat facing him. "And thanks very much for agreeing to see me and for taking time out of what I've discovered is a very busy schedule."

He nodded, and I began preparing to make notes. From there, this is how the interview went, my questions and his answers:

Q. To begin with, what should I call you?

A. Well, what have you heard other people call me?

Q. I've heard different things. And to be honest about it, some of what I've heard strikes me as a little weird.

A. Such as?

Q. I've heard people call you John the Baptist. I suppose they believe you're the Baptist and have come back from the grave. I've also heard people call you Elijah, also come back to

3

life. Or Jeremiah come back. Or some other prophet who has been dead a long time. It's amazing.

A. *(Smiling, as if he couldn't understand it either.)* What would you like to call me? What are you comfortable with?

Q. How about "rabbi"?

A. That's fine.

Q. Or I suppose if I were one of your students, I might call you something like "good master."

A. There is only one who is good. God alone.

Q. Let's settle on "rabbi" then.

A. *(A nod.)*

Q. I'd like you to talk a little about your background. About your family. Your mother and your brothers and sisters. Could you tell me something about them?

A. You saw my mother and my brothers and sisters when you came in just now.

Q. Really? I didn't notice. I met a couple of your students, though. And your hostess, too.

A. They are my family. They are my mother. They are my brothers and sisters. Anyone who is the kind of person my Father wants people to be, that person is my mother. That person is my brother, my sister. People who do the will of my Father are my family.

Q. When you say your "father," who are you are talking about?

A. My Father who is in heaven.

Q. You mean God?

A. I mean the One who sent me here.

Q. Sent you to Bethany?

A. Sent me to this world.

Q. Does that mean you were in some other world before you came here?

A. You, like the others here, are from this world. I'm not. You and the others are of this world. I'm not. I'm from above.

Q. You're from where God is?

A. *(A nod.)*

Q. Tell me about the town where you grew up. Nazareth, wasn't it?

A. Yes. *(A pause.)* It's a town filled with doubt and doubters.

Q. What makes you say that?

A. I was back there not long ago. I had left and had been gone a few years. I returned recently and spoke at the synagogue. I'm afraid the people didn't think much of me.

Q. What happened?

A. They remembered me as the carpenter's son. I guess a carpenter's son isn't supposed to know enough to teach in the synagogue. Anyway, they rejected everything that I had to say. They actually took offense at my teaching.

Q. Do you remember what they said?

A. They seemed a little surprised that I was saying the things I said, and one of them got up and said to the rest of them, "Who is this person, to be spouting off wise sayings and trying to work miracles? Isn't he just the carpenter's son? We know who he is. His mother is Mary. We know her. His brothers are James, Joseph, Simon, and Judas. We know them all. And his sisters, too. They all live around here. This man is nothing special. What does he know?"

Q. So what did you do?

A. There wasn't much I could do. The healing that I had done in other places I wasn't able to do there. I did *some* healings, but not many.

Q. Why not?

A. Miracles of healing require faith. In Nazareth there wasn't enough. The people didn't believe that I could heal them, that I could help them. They refused to believe that I had any authority to instruct them or work miracles. And so I couldn't. I felt powerless there. And of course frustrated.

Q. Was it a case of familiarity breeding contempt?

A. *(A nod.)* A prophet receives honor and respect everywhere except in his own hometown—and among his own relatives.

Q. Did that experience discourage you?

A. It made me sad for a while. But you have to understand that people are going to respond in different ways to what they hear. Not everyone is going to respond with whole-hearted belief. *(A pause.)* There's a little story I like to tell that illustrates my point. A farmer went out into his field to sow

5

seed. As he scattered the seed with his hand, some of the seed fell on the footpath alongside the cultivated area. The birds quickly came and pecked up the seed. Some of the seed fell on places where the soil was shallow, with rocks beneath the topsoil. That seed sprouted, but the sprouts soon withered because there wasn't enough depth for them to grow. Some seed fell among the weeds and thorny bushes at the edge of the field. That seed, too, sprouted, but the weeds and bushes choked them and killed them. Other seed fell on good, fertile soil. And that seed sprouted and grew into plants that produced a bumper crop.

Q. I think I see what you mean.

A. *(A smile.)* If not, you can get one of my students to explain it to you. I've already explained it to them.

Q. Tell me about your students. How did they happen to become your students? Did they apply?

A. I assume you're talking about the twelve.

Q. Right.

A. *(Nodding.)* There are, as perhaps you've noticed, many people who come to hear me teach. Sometimes the number is in the hundreds. At times it's been in the thousands. Some of those people move from place to place with me. Most, though, come and go as they have time and as they are able to be away from their families. Actually, some bring their families with them. But the basic group is the twelve. Some people call them my disciples. They were all handpicked. I handpicked them.

Q. You asked them to come along with you, and they just dropped whatever they were doing and came along?

A. *(Nodding.)* That's pretty much the way it happened.

Q. Can you tell me exactly what you said to them?

A. To some of them, the ones who are fishermen, I said, "Come with me, and I'll have you catching people instead of fish."

Q. And they came.

A. They came.

Q. On what basis did you select them?

A. Potential.

Q. Potential for what?

A. For doing the same things that I do. For doing the things that I'm teaching them to do.

Q. Preaching, teaching, healing, and all that?

A. Yes.

Q. How are they doing so far?

A. *(A smile, then he waggled his hand.)* Some are a little further along than others.

Q. Anyone flunking out?

A. *(Suddenly very serious.)* I don't think I want to answer that. *(A pause.)* We'll just have to see how things go from here on out.

Q. I've made some notes to remind me of the subjects that I want to cover with you. Could we just take them one by one?

A. However you want to do it.

Q. OK. And when you think of something that isn't exactly covered by the question but that you think ought to be said, please just go ahead and say it. And when you can think of examples, illustrations of what you're talking about, please let me have them. Illustrative anecdotes are absolutely precious. From what I've heard about you, you're a marvelous storyteller. So you shouldn't have any trouble or hesitation about telling anecdotes. OK?

A. *(A smile.)* Fine.

His Mission

Q. What would you say is your primary mission? Your main purpose?

A. *(No immediate response.)*

Q. In other words, what's the main reason you're doing what you're doing?

A. If someone has a hundred sheep and one of them manages to wander off alone and get lost, what does the shepherd of that flock do about it? Doesn't he leave the ninety-nine and go off into the wilds to try to find the sheep that's lost?

Q. I suppose so.

A. Yes. And when he finds it, I can tell you he's happier for it than for the ninety-nine who never strayed. He carries that sheep on his shoulders and goes back singing because he's so relieved and happy. And when he sees his friends, he says, "I found it! I found it!" And he feels like throwing a party to celebrate. It's like that with my Father. He doesn't want to lose even one soul. And he rejoices over every one that is recovered.

Q. Are you the shepherd? The searching shepherd?

A. *(A nod.)* I'm here to find and rescue those who are lost.

Q. And who are the lost?

A. My mission is to the lost sheep of the house of Israel.

Q. You're talking about Jews.

A. Yes.

Q. What about non-Jews? They're not part of your search-and-rescue mission?

A. *(A smile.)* Let me tell you about an experience I had recently.

Q. *(Returning the smile.)* That's what I want to hear—an anecdote.

A. *(Still smiling.)* We had left the Galilee area and had walked over to the coast. It's a pretty good distance, as you probably know. About fifty miles. Somewhere between Tyre and Sidon, this woman, a Canaanite woman who lived in this little town, came up to me, frantic, nearly hysterical. "Lord, have pity on me!" she told me, tears streaming from her eyes. "Son of David," she said, "help me! My little girl has a demon in her. She's in absolute misery. Please, do something for her!" For a little while I just stood there and didn't say anything. Some of my students were telling me I should tell her to go away, that she was being a pest. Finally I told the woman, "It's to the Jews that I've been sent, to the house of Israel. I haven't been sent to help Gentiles." When I said that, she dropped to her knees and clasped her hands together. "Please, sir, help me!" I told her, "It wouldn't be right to take the children's food and give it to the dogs." She said, "Yes, but dogs are allowed to eat whatever falls onto the floor from their master's table!" I couldn't resist her. I couldn't resist that kind of sincerity and faith. "Woman," I told her, "your faith is impressive. Get up. Your request is granted."

Q. So what happened to the daughter?

A. She was healed.

Q. Just like that?

A. *(Another smile.)*

Q. Is that still your policy—to deal only with Jews?

A. I have other sheep. Sheep from another fold. I need to bring them in, too. They'll listen to my voice, and when they do, there will be just one flock. One flock, one shepherd.

His Message

Q. What is your message? What is the main point you're trying to get across to people?

A. *(A pause.)* Did you know my cousin John?

Q. The Baptist?

A. Yes.

Q. I never interviewed him. But of course I know about him. He was imprisoned and later executed for saying the wrong things to the wrong persons. Apparently.

A. *(A nod.)* John was the man whom Malachi the prophet was talking about when he said, "Behold, I will send my messenger, and he shall prepare the way before me" (KJV). John showed up in the wilds, preaching to people and telling them, "Get yourselves turned around! Turn around from your lives of sin and self-centeredness and be baptized. If you turn to God, He will forgive you. He will wipe out your guilt and your sin."

Q. I understand that John drew quite a following.

A. *(Nodding.)* People from Jerusalem, from all over Judea, went out there in the wilds to hear him. A lot of people. And large numbers of them, responding to his preaching, confessed their sins and repented. And when they did, John baptized them in the Jordan River.

Q. Someone told me that John baptized you, too. Is that correct?

A. Yes, he did. In the Jordan, just as he baptized the others.

Q. The way I heard it, there was something extraordinary about your baptism. It wasn't *exactly* like the others. Right?

11

A. *(Nodding.)* The moment I came up out of the water, I looked up and saw the heavens burst open, and I saw the Holy Spirit coming down from that opening, like a dove, descending and coming to rest on me. At that point a voice from heaven said to me, "You are my Beloved Son. You are my Delight."

Q. After that, you sort of took over John's job?

A. I spent a long time alone after that. Then after John had been put in prison, I went back to the Galilee area and began preaching the same thing that John had preached. His message and my message were the same. Are the same.

Q. What is it exactly?

A. I am announcing to everyone who will listen that the time has finally come, that the Kingdom of God has at last arrived. I tell them that they should believe what I'm telling them and see it as good news. I tell them they need to get themselves headed in the right direction, away from sin and self-absorption. They need to *do* different and *be* different. They need to turn around and head back to God. John said it, and now I'm saying it. "Repent," he said. "Repent," I say.

Old Ways vs. His Way

Q. Insofar as this repenting, or turning to God, influences a person's life, what he or she does, does it differ from the moral standards that Moses set forth in the laws that he gave us?

A. Let me say first of all that I have not come to do away with the laws of Moses or to nullify the words of the prophets. People shouldn't get the idea that I advocate setting aside *any* of the Scriptures. Far from it. For as long as heaven and earth last, not one part of the law—not even the smallest part, not the dot of an *i*, not the cross of a *t*—is going to be repealed until the whole purpose of the law is accomplished.

Q. So you're not changing the law?

A. Certainly not. If anyone tries to set aside any of the requirements of the law and encourages others to do the same, that person will be counted the very least in the Kingdom of Heaven. By the same token, the person who keeps the law and teaches others to do so will earn for himself or herself a high standing in the Kingdom of Heaven. Let me make it clear: My purpose is not to cancel the laws that Moses set down for us to live by. My purpose is to fulfill those laws—to revitalize them with the meaning that God originally intended.

Q. Can you give me some examples?

A. *(A pause.)* In the past, for many generations, the law has been "You must not commit murder." Anyone who commits murder is required to stand trial and be punished. It was the *act* of murder that was prohibited. Am I not right?

Q. Yes, sir.

A. I am saying now that there's more to evil than the act it-self. I'm saying that if a person stays angry with his brother, he should stand trial. If out of feelings of contempt someone insults his brother, he must face the court. And if someone curses at his brother, he places himself not just in mortal danger but also makes himself liable to the fires of hell.

Q. People say things like that all the time, though, and don't really mean it.

A. *(Nodding.)* That's true, but it's a hurt that needs to be remedied. So if, when you're on your way to worship, you re-alize that someone you know has a grievance against you, go patch up the grievance first and then come back and wor-ship. If a disagreement that you have with someone you know results in a lawsuit against you, you need to settle the lawsuit before the case ever goes to court. That's the way to avoid the severest sort of penalty.

Q. That sounds like a whole new standard of morality.

A. You know what the law says about adultery, don't you?

Q. Yes, I do.

A. Adultery is a prohibited offense. The act of adultery is a violation of the law. But I say that a man doesn't have to commit the act to violate the law. If he looks at a woman and begins thinking he'd like to have sexual relations with her, he is committing adultery with her in his heart. He's guilty even if he never so much as fondles her.

Q. A lot of men would find it hard to avoid that kind of adul-tery.

A. *(Shrugging and gesturing.)* If your eye keeps getting you into trouble, gouge it out and throw it away. It's better to lose one part of your body than to have your whole self dumped into hell. If you can't control your hand, cut the thing off and get rid of it. Again, it's better to suffer the loss of a hand than to suffer the torments of hell.

Q. When you put it that way, it sounds right.

A. One of the old rules was "Don't swear falsely; do what you swore to the Lord you would do." But I'm introducing a new standard: Don't swear at all. Don't use oaths. Don't swear "by heaven," for heaven is the very throne of God.

Don't swear "by earth," for earth is his footstool. Don't swear "by Jerusalem," for it's the city of the great king. Just give a simple "yes" or "no." Anything more than that is playing into the devil's hands.

Q. Yes.

A. As you know, another one of the old rules was "An eye for an eye and a tooth for a tooth." But I say, don't try to get even with the person who wrongs you. If somebody slaps you on the right cheek, offer him your left cheek, too. If somebody sues you for your coat, give him the shirt off your back as well. If somebody forces you to go with him a mile, go two miles. If somebody asks you for something, give it. And if somebody wants to borrow from you, don't turn your back on him or her.

Q. Wow.

A. The old guiding rule was "Love your neighbor and hate your enemy." But what I say is this: Love your enemies. Pray for those who disrespect you and harass you and try to walk all over you. By so doing, you will take on the nature of your heavenly Father, who sends sunshine to both the evil and the good and lets the rain fall on the just and the unjust. If you love only those who love you, what's so great about that? Even disreputable people do that. If you're friendly only to your friends, what's special about that? People who have never even heard of God do that much. No, you are to be completely good, just as God is completely good.

Q. Why haven't we heard teachings like these before?

A. The doctors of the law and the Pharisees—those teachers who insist that everyone must keep the Old Testament law perfectly—are in today's time what Moses was in his time. They have assumed Moses' seat. They have taken on themselves the responsibility of telling you what the law is and interpreting it for you. But I can tell you this, it's better that you should do what they *say* rather than what they *do*. They preach one thing and practice another. The hypocrites! What they like to do is pile up a load of impossible legal demands and place it squarely on everybody else's shoulders, not their own. They wouldn't lift a finger to ease the burden for someone else or share the load. They're a pack of phonies. Everything they do is for show. They wear these supersize phylacteries so that everybody can see them with them on and think how pious they are. They push themselves into front-row seats at ceremonies and sit up on the platform at services so everybody will notice them. They absolutely adore having people bow and scrape to them on the street and call them "rabbi."

Q. *(Smiling.)* You don't seem to have a very high opinion of the doctors of the law and the Pharisees.

A. *(Solemn faced and pointing his finger.)* Let me tell you something. If the religion that a person professes has no better effect on his or her behavior than the religion of the teachers of the law and Pharisees has on *their* behavior, then that person is in deep trouble. There's no way that person is ever going to make it into the Kingdom of Heaven.

Dietary Laws and the Sabbath

Q. While we're on the subject of the law, I understand that you have some radical—or at least, very different—views on our dietary laws. Are they outmoded?

A. You may be thinking of what I've said about eating nonkosher food. *(A pause.)* People are so concerned that what they put into their body may defile them, thinking that they somehow become spiritually and morally unclean from the food they eat. I want people to understand that it's not what they *put into* their mouth that defiles them, that makes them spiritually and morally unclean. What defiles them is what *comes out of* their mouth—their speech and thoughts. What people eat passes through their digestive system and then out of their body. But what *comes out of* their mouth comes from their heart. That's what defiles people. That's what makes them unclean. Out of the heart come all sorts of foul thoughts, murder, adultery, fornication, stealing, lying, slander. That's the kind of thing that defiles people, the thing that makes them spiritually filthy. Eating certain foods or eating with unwashed hands doesn't defile them.

Q. What about the Sabbath laws? Do you think they're too strict?

A. *(A smile.)* I was walking through a wheat field with my students one Sabbath. We had been traveling, and everybody was hungry. So they started plucking the wheat grains from the top of the stalks and were eating them. Well, some Pharisees noticed them doing that, and they were quick to take me to task for it. "Look what your disciples are doing!" they told me. "They're harvesting wheat on the Sabbath! That's a violation of the Sabbath law!"

Q. What did you tell them?

A. I said, "Haven't you ever read in Scripture about what David did when he and his troops were hungry? David went into the temple and ate the ceremonial bread that was supposed to be eaten only by the priests. Talk about breaking the law! He fed it to his men, too. What's more," I said, "don't you know that every Sabbath all priests violate the Sabbath laws? They work on the Sabbath. But they have an excuse."

Q. Did that quiet them?

A. (A shrug.) I told them, "If you knew what this saying means—'What I want from you is mercy, not sacrifice'—you wouldn't be so quick to charge innocent people with breaking the law. The Son of Man, after all, is greater than the Sabbath."

Q. That does seem a commonsense way of looking at the law.

A. Of course. The Sabbath was made for the benefit of people, not people for the Sabbath. (A pause.) Here's an example of the extreme attitude toward Sabbath observance. I was in a synagogue one time, and some Pharisees brought to me this man who had a crippled hand. They let me see him, and then they asked me, "Is it legal to heal on the Sabbath?" I knew what they were up to. They were trying to trap me. I said, "Is there someone here who, if his sheep fell into a pit on the Sabbath, would not grab the sheep and pull it out?" No response. "So isn't a man worth more than a sheep?" I asked them. "So it's legal," I said, "to do good on the Sabbath." And I turned to the man and told him, "Reach out your hand." He did. And his crippled hand was restored. It became just like his other hand.

Q. What did the Pharisees do then?

A. They had nothing to say. But they did go out and plot what they were going to do next.

Genuine Religion

Q. You seem to be saying that religion, genuine religion, is a matter of behavior, not laws. Am I misunderstanding what you're saying? What is it that makes a person's religion genuine?

A. *(Visibly relaxing, a smile momentarily lifting the corners of his mouth.)* I'll tell you another story.

Q. Good.

A. One day when I was with the twelve, I was talking to a group of people, and a lawyer who was in the group stood up and said to me, "Teacher, what do I have to do to make sure I have eternal life?" Now, this was a lawyer, remember. I asked him, "What does the law say? What's your reading of it?" "It says," he answered, "that you must love the Lord your God with all your heart and with all your soul and with all your strength and with all your mind. And you must love your neighbor as much as you love yourself."

Q. A pretty good answer.

A. Yes, it was. And I told him so. "You've answered correctly," I said. "Do as the law says, and you shall have life." Then, looking for the loophole, he said, "Yes, but who *is* my neighbor?" And that led me to another story, one that I told him.

Q. *(Smiling.)* Yes, go on.

A. "There was a man who was traveling from Jerusalem to Jericho," I said, "and on the way he was attacked by a gang of bandits. They beat him senseless, took his money, stripped him of his clothes, and left him lying on the roadside, half dead. And they took off. After a while a clergyman came down the road, and when he was close enough to see the injured man lying there, he crossed over to the other side of the road and kept on going. A little later a temple assistant came by and noticed the robbery victim, still unconscious on the shoulder of the road. He paused briefly to take a good look at the man, then he continued on his way. Later still, a Samaritan came along that same stretch of road. When he saw the man, beat up and bloody, he began to hurt for him. He went over to him and knelt down beside the man. The Samaritan cleansed the wounded man's cuts and abrasions with some wine and oil and then bandaged them. He lifted the man onto his donkey and took him to an inn. He stayed at the inn with the man and tended to him throughout the night. The next morning, when the Samaritan had to leave, he made arrangements with the innkeeper. 'Here's a hundred and fifty dollars,' he said. 'Take care of him, will you? And if his bill runs over the hundred and fifty, I'll make up the difference the next time I see you.'"

Q. Good for him.

A. "Now," I said to the lawyer when I had finished my little tale, "of those three men who happened by, which do you think was a neighbor to the robbery victim?" *(A pause, his eyes fixed on mine, as if he were asking me the question.)*

Q. How did he answer?

A. "The one who showed compassion for the man," he said. He had the right answer. "You're right again," I told him. "Now, you go and do the same."

Q. I think I see what you're saying.

A. *(A smile.)*

Getting Along with Others

Q. It seems that a lot of what you're saying about people and how they're supposed to act has to do with how they interact with other people. I wonder if you have some tips, some guidelines, for getting along with other people.

A. *(Smiling.)* Don't judge people. And you won't be judged. God is going to judge you the same way you judge others. You shouldn't be so eager to point out the little speck that's in somebody else's eye when you've got a huge log in your own eye. It doesn't make sense to say to someone else, "Hold still and let me get that speck out of your eye," before you first remove the board from your own eye. It's hypocritical to pretend you're all right but that the other person isn't. The first thing to do is to eliminate your own problem, and then maybe you can take on somebody else's.

Q. OK.

A. When I was at the temple one morning, I began talking to a whole crowd of people gathered around me. Pretty soon several teachers of the law and Pharisees barged into the group, dragging a woman with them. They stood her there where everybody could see her, and then one of them said to me, "Teacher, this woman has been caught in the act of adultery. Caught in the very act. The law of Moses says that she should be stoned to death. What do *you* say?" *(A pause.)*

Q. What *did* you say?

A. At first I ignored them. I didn't even look at them. I was squatting on the ground, doodling in the sand with my finger. They insisted that I give them an answer. So I stood up and told them, "Let the person who has never sinned cast the first stone." *(Another pause.)* They turned away and left, one by one. The woman was left standing there.

Q. What happened to her?

A. I asked her, "Where are your accusers? Didn't anyone condemn you?" She said, "No, sir." "Neither do I," I told her. "Be on your way. And don't sin anymore."

Q. I see your point. But what happens when somebody does you wrong? Should you simply overlook it?

A. If someone wrongs you, go talk to him or her privately, just the two of you, and discuss the problem. If he sees what you're saying and agrees you have a point, you will have won the person back as a friend. If he refuses to listen, then take one or two others with you as witnesses and go see him again. If that doesn't help, then take the matter to the church. If he won't accept the church's decision, the church should excommunicate him. And I might add that the disposition of the matter, however it's decided, will be as binding in heaven as it is on earth.

Q. And if the person who wronged me acknowledges the wrong and makes amends, what should I do?

A. Forgive him.

Q. What if the person wrongs me again?

A. Forgive again.

Q. How many times can I forgive, though, when somebody keeps taking advantage of me?

A. A great many. Seventy times seven. If in a single day somebody wrongs you seven times and seven times he says he's sorry, forgive him seven times.

Q. But is there any way a person can avoid getting entangled with people who live entirely by a different set of standards or by no standards at all? I'm sure you've run across people like that.

A. All I can tell you is, don't take what's precious and give it to dogs. Don't throw pearls to the pigs. They'll just trample them and then turn on you.

Q. Right.

A. There is one great, guiding principle, one golden rule, that sums up the requirements of the law and the preachings of the prophets, and it concerns just this subject we're talking about.

Q. And what is it?

A. Treat other people the same way you would like them to treat you.

Watching Your Words

Q. I'd guess that watching one's words has a lot to do with a person's getting along with other people. I know that a person's mouth can get him or her into trouble very quickly.

A. A good tree doesn't bear bad fruit. And a bad tree doesn't bear good fruit. Trees are known by the fruit they bear. You can't pick figs off of a thorny hedge, and grapes don't come from bramble bushes. Good people, from the goodness in their heart, bring out good things. Evil people, from the evil in their heart, bring out evil things. Whatever is in a person's heart comes out—and it comes out in his or her speech.

Q. Words *can* hurt you.

A. On Judgment Day a person will have to answer for every careless word he or she has spoken. On that day, your words will either damn you or deliver you.

Q. A scary thought.

A. A person who speaks ill of me can be forgiven. But there is something that cannot be forgiven. Blasphemy against the Holy Spirit will *not* be forgiven. If you speak ill of the Holy Spirit, you will not be forgiven, either in this world or the next.

What He Expects of His Followers

Q. What do you expect from your followers?
A. I tell them that they are the salt of the earth and that they must continue to be so. If salt loses its saltiness, what good is it? It's not fit for anything and might as well be thrown out in the street for people to walk on. I tell my followers that they are the light of the world. They're like a city on a hill. It cannot be hidden when its lights are glowing at night. People don't light a candle and then cover it up with a bushel basket. They put it on a candlestick, where it can shed light on the entire room and everyone in the house can see by it. "Let your light shine out," I tell them, "so that people can see your good deeds and give praise to your heavenly Father for your goodness."
Q. OK.
A. I tell them they are to remember this Scripture verse: "It's mercy I want from you, not sacrifice." I tell them to be careful not to make a big show of making donations or of praying or of fasting. When they make a donation, they're not to let everybody know that they're doing it. That's the way the hypocrites do it, tooting their own horns and calling attention to themselves everywhere. People who do good just because it will make them look good will get the public attention they crave, but that's all they'll get. The way to give is to give secretly—so secretly that your left hand doesn't even know what your right hand is doing. The Father sees that secret deed, and he will reward the giver.
Q. That's something to think about.
A. I tell them that when they pray, don't pray like the hypo-

crites, those people who love to stand up and pray long prayers in the synagogues and on the street corners, where people can see them. They may get some sort of ego gratification out of that, but that's all they're going to get.

Q. How are people supposed to pray?

A. Go off by yourself and pray. Shut the door behind you, and pray in private. And your Father will hear you in private and will reward you. Don't pray the same prayers over and over again. That's what pagans do. They've got the idea that they have to bombard God with their repeated words. Don't do that. After all, I tell people, your Father knows what you need and what you want to pray for before you ever start to pray.

Q. And what about fasting?

A. When you fast, again, don't do it the way the hypocrites do it. They put on this long, sad face *(demonstrating it)* and try to make themselves look as miserable as possible—all so that other people will know they're really suffering and they're so devout. Whatever admiration they get from others is all they're going to get for that. The way to fast is to wash your face, comb your hair, look as you normally do, no matter how empty you feel in your stomach. Other people won't know you're fasting. But your Father will know, and he will reward you.

Q. Do you really expect all of your followers, everyone who has responded to your preaching, to do everything you're asking them to do? To be what you're telling them they should be?

A. Well, not everyone who keeps on saying to me, "Lord, Lord," is going to make it into the Kingdom of Heaven. The only ones who'll make it are the ones who actually *do* the will of my Father in heaven. When the time comes, a lot of people will say to me, "Lord, Lord, didn't we preach sermons and teach about you? Didn't we heal people and do a lot of other good things in your name?" And I'll simply tell them, "Get out of here. I don't know you. You've not worked for me. You worked for the cause of evil."

Q. Isn't that a pretty hard judgment?

A. *(A shrug.)* Everyone has his or her opportunities to make the right choices. Everyone who listens to what I'm saying and puts my words into practice is like the man who with good sense built his house on a foundation of rock. When the rainstorms flooded the area and the storm winds beat against the house, it withstood the floods and the winds because it was built on a solid foundation. But everyone who hears what I'm saying and disregards my words is like the very foolish man who built his house on sand. When the hard rains flooded the property and the storm winds started blowing, the house collapsed with a horrible crash.

Q. A natural outcome.

A. Or go back to my story about the farmer who scattered his seed and some of it grew up into thriving plants and some didn't. Here's the explanation of that story. The hard path beside the field, where some of the seed landed, represents those people who hear the message about the Kingdom of Heaven and don't understand it. Satan comes along and snatches the message from their hearts, like a bird eating up seed. The shallow topsoil with the layer of rock beneath it represents those who accept the message and do so happily. But when tough times come, when doubts come, when their faith starts to present problems, their commitment quickly fades and they drop out. The ground with thorny bushes and weeds represents people who hear the message but are too concerned with having a comfortable lifestyle and keeping up with their neighbors. For them the message is choked out, crowded out by *things* and the pursuit of more things. The good, fertile soil represents those people who listen carefully to the message, understand it, heed it, and then go out and bring others to the Kingdom—thirty others, sixty, even a hundred others.

Q. Does that mean you expect your followers to produce other followers?

A. The time is coming when I will tell my students, my disciples, "Go out and make disciples in nations all over the world. Baptize them in the name of the Father, the Son, and the Holy Spirit. And teach them to follow the same rules, obey the same commandments, that I have given you." *(A pause.)*

I'll also assure them that I'll be with them. I'll always be with them, until the end of the world.

Q. That's a lot to think about. You've touched on a number of things—including the end of the world. I'm interested in hearing you talk more about that later on. Now I'd like you to talk about something that I have here in the notes that I made to myself.

A. Go ahead.

What Is God Really Like?

Q. I think a lot of people have the idea that God is this un-knowable, awesome being who is to be feared. They think we should be afraid to offend him because he will deal harshly with us if we do. Also, there is the idea that God *wants* us to fear him. I wish you would tell me how you see God. What is he really like? How do you characterize him?

A. *(A long pause.)* A few months ago my students and I were passing through Samaria, on our way to the Galilee area. We came to the outskirts of a little town called Sychar. It's near the property that the patriarch Jacob gave to his son Joseph. It's a historic area. There's a well there, a spring that's called Jacob's Well.

Q. Right. I know the place.

A. We stopped at the well, and my students then went on into the town to get us something to eat. But I stayed at the well. I was tired and hot from all the walking we had done, and I decided just to take a break. It was about noon. While I was sitting there, a woman came to the well to draw water. "I'd be grateful," I told her, "if you'd give me a drink of your water." The woman acted shocked. "How is it that you, obviously a Jew, are asking me, a Samaritan woman, to give you a drink? Jews don't speak to Samaritans or have anything to do with us."

Q. True.

A. *(A nod.)* I told her, "If you knew what a wonderful gift God can give to you and who it is that's asking you for water, you would ask him to give you 'living water.' And he would give it to you." She said, "You don't have anything to draw water with. You don't have a rope; you don't have a bucket. And this is a deep well. So where are you going to get this 'living water'? Do you think you're a better man than our forefather Jacob, who took his water from this well and drank it and gave it to his children and his cattle to drink as well?" I told her, "Everyone who drinks from this well will be thirsty again. But everyone who drinks the kind of water I'm talking about will never thirst again. The kind of water that I can give is itself an artesian well, a spring from which eternal life gushes." "Sir," she said, "please give me some of that water so I'll never be thirsty again or have to come here and haul water up out of this well."

Q. Smart woman.

A. *(A smile.)* "Go get your husband," I told her. "And then come back here." "I don't have a husband," she told me. "You're right about that," I said. "You've had five husbands, but the man you're living with now is somebody you never married." She said, "You must be some kind of prophet. So let me ask you something. In spite of the fact that our ancestors worshiped God here on this mountain, you Jews insist that Jerusalem is the place to worship. What about that?"

Q. What did you tell her?

A. I told her the same thing I am about to tell you, in answer to your earlier question.

Q. Good.

A. I told her, "God is Spirit."

Q. Not a creature, not an object.

A. "And so in order to worship God," I told her, "you must worship him with your spirit. And you must worship him with sincerity. Because that's the sort of worship the Father requires. The time is coming when people will no longer worship the Father either on this mountain, as you're accustomed to doing, or in Jerusalem; they'll realize that it's not necessary to go to a certain place to worship him. As for the Jews, they are God's vehicle for salvation," I said, "and they know full well who it is that they're worshiping. You evidently don't know." She said, "I know that the Messiah, the

Christ, is going to come and that he is going to tell us everything we need to know. I know that much." "I'm the Messiah," I told her. *(Another pause.)*

Q. What did she say to that?

A. Just about that time, my students returned. They seemed surprised that I was talking to the woman, but nobody asked me why I was talking to her or what we had been talking about. They urged me to eat the food that they had brought for me, but I told them, "No, thanks, I've had my nourishment." They were a little puzzled, and so I told them, "My food is doing the will of him who sent me and bringing his work to completion." While I was telling them that, the woman left her water pot by the well and went into town and started telling everybody, "Come see this man who told me everything I've ever done in my whole life. He must be the Christ!" So a big crowd of townspeople came streaming out to the well to get a look. They persuaded me to spend some time in their town, talking with them, and I ended up staying there two days. There were a lot of decisions made. *(A pause.)* Now let me go to the heart of your question of what God is really like by telling you another story. I believe you'd call it an illustrative anecdote. *(Smiling.)*

Q. Please go ahead.

A. A man had two sons, and one day the younger boy came to his father and said, "Father, eventually you're going to leave me part of your estate. But I don't want to have to wait for it, and I'd like you to divide up the property now and let me have what's coming to me." The father went along with his son's request, and a few days later the young man packed his bags, took his money, and left. He traveled a long way and finally reached a big city, where he started throwing his money around. It wasn't long before he had gone through his entire inheritance, partying and living high and otherwise wasting the money. Then, when he was flat broke, hard times hit. The whole area was struck by a famine, and the young man was about to starve to death. He managed to get himself a job taking care of a farmer's pigs, but the pay was so poor that to stay alive he had to eat the bean pods and the other things the pigs were eating. At that point he finally came to his senses and realized what a mess he had made of his life. He took a look at the squalor and filth around him and said to himself, "My father's hired hands are living a lot better than I am. It's crazy for me to go on like this. I'm going back to my father and admit to him that I made a big mistake. I'll tell him I know that I've forfeited my right to be called a son of his, but I'll beg him to give me a job as a hired man. Maybe he will." So he got up out of the pigpen and made his way back to his father's place. When he was still a distance away, his father spotted him coming across the fields. The father recognized the boy and ran out to meet him. When he reached his son, the father grabbed the young man in his arms and hugged his neck and kissed his cheeks. "My son! My son!" And the son told him, "Father, I know I've sinned against heaven and against you. I don't deserve to be called your son." "Don't talk like that," his father told him and then turned to a couple of the hired hands who had followed him when they saw him running. "Go back to the house," he told them, "and bring the best robe you can find and put it on my son. Get a ring and put it on his finger. Get some shoes and put them on my boy's feet. And butcher that calf we've been fattening up and roast it, and let's have a feast and celebrate. My son is back! He was dead, but he's alive again! He was lost, but now he's been found! I've got my son back again!" So they had this big party. Meanwhile, the older son, who had been out in a distant pasture, was coming back to the house. When he got close, he heard music and people laughing, and he wondered what was going on. He called over one of the servants and asked him what it was all about. "Your brother has come back, and your father has butchered that calf we've been fattening, and he's throwing a party to celebrate your brother's safe return." The older brother then suddenly became angry, and he refused to go inside to the party. His father came out to talk to him, to persuade him to come join the festivities. "No, sir," the son said. "All these years I've worked long and hard for you. I've done everything you ever asked me. Not once did I ever disobey you. But I never got a party. I never got so much as a baby goat that I could share with my friends. But this—this son of yours who turned his back on you and blew your money messing around with a bunch of women in the city, he comes back here, and you kill the calf and give a big party for him!" Then the father said, "Son, I know you've been a faithful and dutiful son. And, believe me, I'm devoted to you. Everything I have is yours. But it's only right that we have a celebration for your brother. Don't you understand? It's as if he were dead and now he's alive again. He was lost to us, but now we've found him." *(A smile, his arms held out, like the father's in the story.)*

Q. And you're saying that God is like that father, that forgiving father.

A. *(Still smiling.)*

The Necessity for Forgiveness

Q. Forgiveness seems to be a recurring theme in what you're saying, in the stories you tell. Is it something you emphasize?

A. *(Nodding.)* If you forgive others when they wrong you, your heavenly Father will forgive you when you do wrong. But if you refuse to forgive the other person, your heavenly Father will refuse to forgive you. There's a story that illustrates the principle.

Q. OK.

A. A king was going over his account books one day and noticed that one of his managers owed him a debt that had accumulated to twenty million dollars. The king called in the manager and demanded payment. And when the manager said he was unable to pay, the king ordered not only that the man, his wife, and his children be sold into slavery but also that all of his property be seized and sold to satisfy the debt. The manager fell on his knees before the king and pleaded with him. "My lord, please, be patient with me. I will pay. Every last dollar. I promise. Just give me some time. Please." The king felt sorry for him then and canceled the entire debt. On his way out of the king's palace, the manager ran into another of the king's employees, a man who owed the manager two thousand dollars. The manager grabbed the man by the throat and told him, "Pay me what you owe me!" The man began begging for more time. "I'll pay you, but I need more time to get the money together. Please be patient with me." But the manager refused and had the man arrested and thrown into debtor's prison. Some of the king's servants witnessed what had happened and were so upset about it that they went and told the king. The king summoned the manager. "You miserable, rotten ingrate," the king told him, "I forgave you your entire debt because you begged me to and I felt sorry for you. Shouldn't you have had pity for your debtor in the same way I had pity for you?" The king was so furious that he ordered the manager imprisoned and tortured until he paid off the twenty million dollars.

Q. And the lesson is . . .

A. My heavenly Father will do the same to you if in your heart you do not forgive people who have wronged you.

Q. Have you seen it work the way it's supposed to? Someone who has been forgiven does then go and show similar pity for someone else?

A. One time I was invited to dinner by a Pharisee, and I accepted his invitation and went home with him. We were at the table eating when a woman came in. The woman was a notorious figure in town, a woman with a really bad reputation. She had heard that I was at this Pharisee's house, and she was determined to see me. So she managed to make her way into the room. She had with her an alabaster flask with perfume in it. She knelt behind me and started crying, copiously, so much so that her tears were falling on my feet. So she began wiping and washing my feet with her tears and drying them with her hair. She kissed them and then poured the perfumed oil from her flask onto my feet to soothe them.

Q. What did the Pharisee think of all that?

A. I could read his mind. He was saying to himself, *This just proves that this Jesus is no real prophet. If he were, he'd know the kind of woman this creature is.* So I said to him, "Simon, let me tell you something." "Please do," he said. Then I told him a story. "There was a moneylender who had two men who owed him money and were behind in their payments. One owed him ten thousand dollars, and the other owed him a hundred dollars. Neither one could pay, and the moneylender decided to cancel both debts. Now then," I asked my host, "of the two whose debts he forgave, which one do you think will love him most?" He said, "I guess the one who owed the most."

Q. That would be my answer, too.

A. *(A nod.)* "You're right," I told him. Then I turned toward the woman and said, "Simon, do you see this woman? I came into your house, and you didn't trouble yourself to offer me water to wash my feet. But this woman has washed my feet with her tears and has wiped them with her hair. You neglected to greet me with a kiss, but this woman has repeatedly kissed my feet. You didn't bother to anoint my head with olive oil. But she has anointed my feet with perfume. Therefore, I'm telling you this: Her sins—and there are a lot of them—are forgiven, for she has loved much. But the person who has been forgiven of little, that person shows very little love."

Q. What happened to the woman then?

A. I told her, "Your sins are forgiven." And when I said that, the other guests at the table said to each other, "Who does this guy think he is, saying he is forgiving people's sins?" But I told the woman, "Your faith has saved you. Go in peace."

The Importance of Faith

Q. In that last story you said that the woman's faith saved her. Earlier on you said that faith is essential in healing. Would you elaborate on the subject of faith and how it affects a person's life?

A. As I once told my students, if you have faith—even an amount no bigger than a mustard seed—and if there's not a doubt in your heart, you could say to the Mount of Olives, "Move yourself from where you are to that spot over there," and it would do it. If you have faith, nothing is impossible.

Q. Do you remember the occasion when you told them that? Was there something that brought that on?

A. *(A nod.)* I remember it clearly. I had gone up on the mountaintop and had taken Peter, James, and John—three of my most serious students—with me. When we came back down, we found a crowd waiting. As we came nearer, a man stepped out of the crowd and fell on his knees in front of me and said, "Lord, have pity on my son. He's tortured by seizures. Several times when he has had these seizures, he has fallen into the fire or into the water. I brought him to your disciples, but they couldn't heal him." My first reaction was to say to my students, "What a stubborn and doubtful bunch of people you are! How long will it take for me to get through to you?" Then I said, "Bring the boy to me." I rebuked the demon in the boy, and it left him. After that, he was cured. Later my students came and asked me, "Why couldn't we cure the boy?"

Q. What did you tell them?

A. I said, "Because you didn't really believe it could be done."

Q. That must have made them think hard. What are some other examples of faith that you've seen?

A. *(A pause.)* I was in Capernaum one time, and a Roman army officer who had heard about me sent a delegation of Jewish elders to me, urging me to come and heal one of his slaves, a man of whom the officer was particularly fond. The slave was extremely ill and at the point of death. The delegation of elders pleaded with me on behalf of the officer. "He really deserves your help," they told me. "He's been a good friend to our people. He built us a new synagogue." So I started to go with them to where the officer lived. On the way there, I was intercepted by a group of his friends. The officer had sent them to deliver a message to me. This is what he had told them to tell me: "Lord, I don't want to put you to the trouble of having to come all the way to my house. And besides, I don't feel that I'm good enough to have you as my guest in my house. I don't feel worthy even to come face-to-face with you. So if you will just say the word, speak it from where you are, my servant will be healed. I know it because I'm used to giving orders myself. I tell my men, 'Go,' and they go. I tell them, 'Come,' and they come. I tell my slave, 'Do this,' and he does it. So if you will just give the order, my servant will be made well." I was really impressed with that officer. So much so that I turned around to my students and the throng that was tagging along behind us and I told them, "Never in my life have I run across faith like this before, not in Israel, not anywhere."

Q. And was the officer's slave healed then?

A. Yes, and by the time the officer's friends got back, the slave became entirely well.

Q. Any other outstanding experience of faith that you remember?

A. Another time when I was in Capernaum, I was speaking at the home of friends. The house became so crowded with people that there was no more room to fit them in. Even the doorway was filled. It was standing room only. While I was preaching to the crowd, we heard a noise and a commotion up on the roof. When we looked up, we saw a hole begin to open up in the ceiling of the room. There were four men up there on the roof, removing tile from the roof until finally they had made an opening big enough for them to lower a sleeping mat down through it. Down the mat came through the opening, and on it was a man who was paralyzed. The four men wanted me to heal him.

Q. So what happened?

A. I was so moved by their demonstration of faith that I immediately said to the man, "Son, your sins are hereby forgiven." That set off some bad thoughts among the teachers of the law who were in the crowd. They started asking themselves, *Why does he say things like that? That's blasphemy! Only God can forgive sin.*

Q. Did you say anything to them?

A. I asked them, "Why do you have to fight what I say? After all, what is easier for me to say to this paralyzed man—'Your sins are forgiven' or 'Get up, pick up your mat, and walk'? Just to show you that the Son of Man has the power on earth to forgive sins, I will do what is apparently more difficult." I turned to the paralyzed man and told him, "Stand up, pick up your mat, and go home. You are healed."

Q. And then what happened?

A. *(A smile.)* The man got to his feet, lifted his mat, and squeezed out as the crowd of onlookers pressed back to let him pass. There were a lot of amazed and happy people in the crowd at that point. They broke out into a chorus of hallelujahs.

Q. I wish I had been there.

A. Another person of unusual faith is a woman who had suffered from a mysterious hemorrhage for twelve years. She had been to all kinds of doctors and had gone broke paying their bills. On top of that, none of them had been able to do anything for her. She was in the crowd that was walking along with me while I was on my way to heal someone else, a very sick little girl. There were people everywhere, in the road and alongside it. But suddenly, while I was walking, I had a feeling that something had been released from me, and I asked the people near me, "Who touched my clothes?" A couple of my students said it was impossible to tell. "All these people crowding you, and you ask who touched you?" But I kept looking around, and my eyes landed on this woman, who now was stricken with fear, afraid that she had done something terribly wrong. She came up to me, confessed that she had touched me, and told me her whole story. She had simply touched my cloak. That was all she had meant to do. She had told herself, "If I can just touch his clothing, just his clothing, I know I'll be healed."

Q. And had she been healed?

A. She had. The hemorrhaging had stopped immediately. She could tell it.

Q. Amazing. And what did you tell her after she confessed?

A. I said, "Daughter, it's your faith that has made you well. Go in peace, forever healed of your ailment."

Q. That's quite a story.

A. There are a lot of others.

Q. I wish we had time for you to tell them all. They'd probably make a book. But I know you don't have the time. Could we talk about how faith or belief affects a person in ways other than in healing?

A. Faith has effects in prayer.

Q. OK. I'd like to come back a little later to the subject of prayer. What else besides prayer?

A. When the good news of the coming of the Kingdom of Heaven is preached and people hear it, everyone who believes and is baptized will be saved. On the other hand, the person who does not believe stands condemned. *(A pause.)* Let me tell you about my experience with a man named Nicodemus. I'm suddenly reminded of him, and my conversation with him has a bearing on the subject of faith and belief.

Q. All right.

A. Nicodemus was—is—a Pharisee and a member of the Sanhedrin, and one night he came to the house where I was staying so that we could have a talk. "Rabbi," he said, "everybody knows that you are a teacher sent to us by God. Nobody can do the things you do, the miracles you do, unless God is with him." I could see where he was going, and I said to him, "I want to tell you as earnestly as I can that unless you are born again, you will never make it into the Kingdom of Heaven." "How is that possible?" he said. "How can a grown man be born? Are you saying that he can reenter his mother's womb and be born all over again?" I told him, "Listen closely to me. This is important. I am saying that unless a person is born both physically and spiritually, he or she cannot enter the Kingdom of Heaven. Flesh comes from flesh. Spirit comes from spirit. You shouldn't act dumbfounded when I tell you about being born again. The wind blows as it wills, and you know about it only because of its effects. You can hear it, but you can't tell where it's coming from or where it's going. It's the same way with everyone who is born by the Spirit. You can't explain the phenomenon, but you can tell the effects of it."

Q. I guess it is difficult to grasp.

A. Nicodemus thought so. "I don't know how that can be," he told me. I said, "You, a learned teacher of Israel, say you don't know what I'm talking about? Let me assure you that we are talking about something that we *do* know about. We are witnessing to something we have actually observed. And can't you believe me? If I'm telling you about things that occur here on earth and you don't believe what I'm saying, how will I be able to tell you about things in heaven and have you believe me? There is only one who has been to heaven and seen it. He is the same one who has come to earth from heaven. It is I, the Son of Man. Just as Moses lifted up the bronze serpent in the wilderness so that the people could look up and be saved, the Son of Man must be lifted up, too, so that everyone who believes in me will not die but will have eternal life. For God loved the world so much that he sent his only Son from heaven to earth so that anyone who believes in the Son will not die but will have everlasting life. The person who believes is not condemned, but the person who doesn't believe *is* condemned." *(A long pause.)*

Q. So belief, or faith, is extremely important to everyone. It's vital.

A. Anyone who believes in me is not believing in *me;* he or

45

she is believing in the One who sent me. Believers don't see *me;* they see the One who sent me. I've come like a light into the world so that whoever believes in me will not have to live in darkness. If people hear what I'm saying and reject my words, it's not I who will ultimately judge them—for I didn't come to judge the world but rather to save it. People who reject me and reject my words will indeed have a judge, however. The very words that I have spoken will be their judge on the last day. I do not say things on my own authority. The Father who sent me gave me strict instructions and told me what I should say; he told me the words I should speak. And I know that what he orders means eternal life. So whatever he orders me to say, I say.

Q. You are God's representative.

A. The Father and I are one. If you've seen me, you've seen the Father. People may either believe me when I say that I am in the Father and the Father is in me, or they may believe on the basis of what I've done and am doing. But I can tell you this, those who believe in me will be able to do the same things I do, if not even greater things, once I've returned to the Father.

Q. That's a lot to digest.

A. *(A nod.)*

46

Prayer

Q. Let's return to the subject of prayer, since we so recently touched on it. What have you taught your students about prayer?

A. One day after I had been praying, one of them came to me and said, "Lord, John the Baptist used to teach his disciples how to pray. Would you teach us to pray?" I told them, "When you pray, say: 'Our Father in heaven, hallowed be your name, your kingdom come, your will be done on earth as it is in heaven. Give us today our daily bread. Forgive us our debts, as we also have forgiven our debtors. And lead us not into temptation, but deliver us from the evil one'" (NIV).

Q. What principles of prayer should people follow?

A. Have complete faith in God. Have no doubt in your heart. Whatever you pray for, believe that you are receiving it, and you will receive it.

Q. How about attitude? Does a person need a certain attitude, besides having faith?

A. When you start to pray and you realize that you have bad feelings toward someone, forgive that person right then and there. Don't hold on to your bad feelings.

Q. Ah. The forgiveness theme again.

A. Yes.

Q. Are there any limits to what a person may ask for when he or she prays?

A. If you stay close to me and let my words stay alive in you, you may ask anything you want in my name, and it will be done for you. If any two of my followers agree on something

47

that they should pray for, whatever it is, their prayer will be answered by my Father in heaven. Because where two or three of them are drawn together in my name, I'm right there with them.

Q. What if people are not sure if they should ask for something?

A. What do they have to lose? Ask, and you'll receive. Seek, and you will find. Knock, and the door will be opened for you. The one who asks receives. The one who seeks finds. The one who knocks has the door opened. Remember this, if a child asks his father for a piece of bread, will the father give him a rock? If the child asks for a fish to eat, will the father give her a snake? Of course not. So if humans, with all their faults and failings, can care enough to give their children good things when they ask for them, isn't it easy enough to believe that your Father in heaven will care even more to give good things to his children when they ask?

Q. Indeed.

A. Another principle is to keep praying. Be persistent in your praying. Don't get discouraged, and don't give up. *(A pause.)* I'll tell you a story that I told my students when I was trying to make the same point to them.

Q. All right.

A. In a certain city there was a hard-nosed judge who had little sympathy for other people and no regard at all for God. In the same city was a widow who had a grievance against a man she believed had cheated her, and she came to the judge pleading for help. "Give me justice," she begged him. He ignored her plea. But she kept coming back to him, urging him to consider her case and grant her relief. Time after time, she came back to the judge with her appeal. Finally he said, "I'm not afraid of God, and I don't really care much about people, but this woman is such a pest that I'm going to make it my business to see that she gets justice in this case. She's wearing me out with all her constant petitions." Now, if a judge like that can be moved by persistent pleading, isn't it reasonable to believe that God will grant relief to his people when they persist in their prayers?

Q. I should say so.

A. I do have a caution to offer about praying.

Q. What is it?

A. It concerns a person's attitude. Some people think they've earned the right to assault God's ears with self-righteous prayers. At the same time, they think that those who are less righteous than they are don't deserve to be heard by God. That's a really bad attitude. I have a story that speaks to the problem. *(Smiling.)*

Q. I'm all ears.

A. Two men went into the temple to pray. One was a Pharisee; the other was one of those despised tax collectors. The Pharisee stood and started praying. "Lord, I want to thank you that I'm not like other men—thieves, swindlers, crooks, men who cheat on their wives, or somebody like this tax collector. I fast twice a week, and I give my tithe regularly." Meanwhile, the tax collector, standing a distance from the Pharisee, too timid even to raise his eyes toward heaven, beat himself on the chest in an expression of remorse and prayed this prayer: "God, be merciful to me, a sinner." I want to tell you that the tax collector was the one who went home with God's forgiveness, not the Pharisee. People who exalt themselves are eventually going to be brought down, and people who humble themselves are going to be exalted.

Phony Religion

Q. From what you've said about Pharisees, I take it that you have strong feelings toward our religious leaders.

A. So many of the Pharisees are hypocrites. They're playactors. Their religion isn't real. It's all an act. While they're pretending to be so holy, praying their long, pious prayers in public, they're at the same time foreclosing on the homes of widows and forcing them out onto the street. They're such sticklers for the letter of the law, but they ignore the spirit of it. They pay their tithes regularly, down to the tenth little mint leaf that grows in their window boxes, but they are completely oblivious to what's really important in the requirements of the law.

Q. Such as?

A. Such as justice. Such as mercy. Such as faith.

Q. Tithing's not important?

A. Certainly it's important. They ought to tithe. But giving a tithe is no excuse for ignoring what's even more important. The religious phonies are ever so careful to strain a gnat out of their soup, but then they'll swallow a camel whole. They're so meticulous about getting the outside of the cup and dish clean and shiny, but they leave the inside filthy with their extortion and greed and self-indulgence. They need first of all to clean up the mess on the *inside* of the cup and then, after that, when they polish the outside, they'll have a whole cup that's clean. *(A pause.)* I'll tell you what the religious phonies are like. They're like whitewashed tombs. You've been to the cemetery and seen how people whitewash the family tombs to beautify them?

Q. Yes.

A. Religious phonies are like those tombs. When they're

whitewashed, the tombs look very nice on the outside, spar-
kling white, neat and clean. But inside, that's another matter.
Inside they're full of decay. They're full of death, bones, and
rotting flesh. Religious phonies are the same way. They look
nice and saintly out in public, but beneath that outward appearance, behind that public show, beats a heart blackened
and corrupt with all kinds of disgusting hypocrisy and foul
wrongdoing.

Q. But are they really hurting anyone besides themselves?

A. They're barring the door to the Kingdom of Heaven. They're
preventing others from entering at the same time that they're
keeping themselves out. They are like blind guides. They knock
themselves out to recruit others to their ideas of religion. And
when they find people who accept their misguided laws, they
make them twice the sons and daughters of hell that they are.
These people shouldn't be called "rabbi." There's only one
rabbi, one teacher. Everyone else is a brother or sister. And no
one on earth should be called "Father." There is just one Father,
and he is in heaven. *(A pause.)* I'll tell you a story that makes a
point about our religious leaders.

Q. OK.

A. A man who had two sons went to one of them and said,
"Son, I want you to work in my vineyard today." The son told
him, "No, I don't want to." But later the son changed his mind
and went and worked in the vineyard as his father had asked
him. The man also told his other son, "Son, I want you to work
in the vineyard today." The second son told his father, "Yes,
sir. I'll do it." But he never did. Now then, which of the two
sons did the will of his father?

Q. The first one.

A. That's exactly right. And I'll tell you this, tax collectors
and prostitutes will enter the Kingdom of God before those
religious leaders ever do. John the Baptist came and
preached the way of right living to them, and they spurned
his words. But the tax collectors and prostitutes heard him
and believed his message of repentance. And even when the
religious leaders saw the conversion of sinners, they still refused to accept John's call to repentance.

The Humble, the Arrogant, and the Stubborn

Q. You seem to have an affinity for ordinary, humble people and an aversion for people who are arrogant and pushy.

A. I was invited to dinner not long ago, and when I got to the home of my host, I found that he had invited quite a few other people, too. One of the first things I noticed was how so many of the other guests were trying to grab seats at the head table. I offered them a suggestion. "It's much more becoming to you, and a lot safer as well, to take a seat far from the head table. If you seat yourself at the head table and you're not supposed to be there, you'll have to suffer the embarrassment of being told to get up and move so that the person who is supposed to sit there may have the seat. But if you sit in a less desirable seat in the first place and the host wants you at the head table, he'll come and get you and usher you into a place of honor. Believe me, it's a lot better that way." People who are so eager to be first will end up being last, and those who are willing to place themselves last will end up being first.

Q. Do you tend to identify more with ordinary people than with the high and mighty?

A. In the book of Isaiah you will find these words: "The Spirit of the Sovereign Lord is upon me, because the Lord has appointed me to bring good news to the poor. He has sent me to comfort the brokenhearted and to announce that captives will be released and prisoners will be freed. He has sent me to tell those who mourn that the time of the Lord's favor has come." *(A pause.)* I'm here to make those words come true.

Q. From that, it sounds as if God gives special consideration to humble, ordinary people.

A. The humble people of this earth are blessed. The Kingdom of Heaven is going to be theirs. Those who have suffered deep grief and known great sorrow are blessed. They're going to receive the ultimate comfort. People who are sweet-natured and gentle are blessed. They're going to inherit the earth. People who are hungry for goodness are blessed. Their appetite for goodness is going to be completely satisfied. People whose hearts are filled with mercy are blessed. They're going to receive abundant mercy themselves. People who are wholly sincere and totally without guile are blessed. They're going to be able to see the very face of God. People who are peacemakers are blessed. They are going to be known as God's very own children because they're so much like him. People who suffer ridicule and scorn and persecution—who are lied about and laughed at because they are living lives that God has told them to live—are blessed. Such people should be especially happy because their reward in heaven is going to be extraordinary. They stand in the shoes of the prophets, who were persecuted in similar ways and for similar reasons.

Q. What about the others?

A. They—the doctors of the law, the Pharisees, all the hypocrites—are in for a lot of grief. They build shrines and monuments to the murdered prophets, and they put wreaths and flowers on the graves of godly men and women, and they say, "If we had been alive during the times of our ancestors, we certainly would never have done what they did, persecuting and killing God's spokesmen the way they did. It was awful!" They readily admit that they are the sons of those who murdered the prophets. I say to them, "Yes, you're their sons. And you're following their example. Like father, like son." They're a bunch of snakes. They're the offspring of vipers. There is no way that they're going to escape damnation in hell. In time, when I commission and send out preachers and teachers and writers, these hypocrites will crucify and kill some of them and flog others in their synagogues and drive them out of town and harass them from one place to the next. From the hands of these foul snakes drips the blood of every good man and woman who has ever been persecuted and murdered—every last one of them, from the sweet and innocent Abel, who was slain by his brother, to Zechariah son of Barachiah, the man they were brazen enough to murder in the temple itself, between the sanctuary and the altar. The entire weight of responsibility for those crimes will fall on today's generation.

Q. How does that make you feel, knowing that that kind of judgment is going to be meted out to these people?

A. *(Holding his hand to his forehead and shaking his head.)* Jerusalem! Jerusalem! What a place! It's the city that murders prophets. It's the city that stones everyone God sends to speak to it. How many times I have yearned to put my arms around its people, to gather them to me as a mother hen gathers her chicks under her wings! But they wouldn't let me. They didn't want any part of me. Now their city will become just an empty house. I'm not going to have anything more to do with it until it's ready to proclaim, "Blessed is he who comes in the name of the Lord!"

Money and Wealth

Q. From what you say about poor people, about the under-privileged and about ordinary people, I get the feeling that you view money and wealth as a handicap to faith. Is it?

A. Well, I'll tell you this—it's easier for a camel to go through the eye of a needle than it is for a rich person to enter the Kingdom of God.

Q. Is that a little bit of an exaggeration?

A. *(A brief smile.)* Nobody can serve two masters. Anyone who tries will either hate one and love the other or be loyal to one and disregard the other. You just cannot serve both God and money.

Q. So you're saying that pursuing wealth is incompatible with pursuing God.

A. *(Nodding.)* People shouldn't be so concerned about stacking up wealth or acquiring property here on earth. Whatever they gain here is subject to loss of one kind or another. Instead, they should be concerned about accumulating wealth in heaven. That's the place to make your investment. There's no danger of loss there. Here's the principle: Wherever you have your treasure, that's where you're also going to have your heart.

Q. Whatever is important to a person is what he or she is going to be particularly interested in. Is that it?

A. The things that people think are important God is likely to consider an abomination. *(A pause.)* The wealthy have it good now. Their money's buying them a lot of comfort. But things are going to be different for them in the future. They're going to experience a dramatic reversal of fortune. They're going to go from riches to rags.

Q. *(Smiling.)* Do you, by any chance, have a story that goes along with that?

A. Actually I do. I was talking to a large group one day, and a man in the crowd asked me for a favor. "Teacher, I would appreciate it if you would tell my brother that he should divide the inheritance we got from our father and give me my share." "Sir, I'm afraid you have the wrong idea about me," I told him. "Nobody made me a judge or arbitrator over your family's money squabbles." I told the people in the crowd, "Every one of you, think about what you're doing with your life. Getting things and accumulating money isn't what life is all about." Then I told them a little story. *(A quick smile.)* "A wealthy planter, whose land had already made him a fortune, was having a banner year. 'What am I going to do with all this produce?' he asked himself. 'My barns are already full. There's no room to store anything else.' Then he had what he thought was a brilliant idea. 'I've got it!' he said. 'I'll tear down my barns and build bigger ones, big enough to hold everything. After that, I'll be in good shape. I'll have enough to last me a very long time. I can take it easy and enjoy myself.' But God had a different idea, a different plan for the planter. 'You're a fool,' God told him. 'Tonight you will die, and I will come demanding your soul. Then what's going to happen to all your precious fortune?'" I told the crowd, "Anyone who concentrates on earthly wealth instead of a rich relationship with God is just as big a fool as that wealthy planter."

Q. Have you actually run into people for whom wealth is a barrier to living the way you're saying a person should live?

A. *(A nod.)* A young man came up to me one day and asked me, "What do I have to do to gain eternal life?" It's a question I'm often asked. I told this young man, "If you want eternal life, keep the commandments." "Which ones?" he asked me. I told him, "Don't murder. Don't commit adultery. Don't steal. Don't give false testimony. Honor your father and mother. And love your neighbor as much as you love yourself." "I've been keeping all those commandments ever since I was a boy," he said, "but I feel that I'm missing something. What is it?" I could see what his real problem was. I told him, "If you want to do everything you should, go sell everything you've got and give the money to the poor. That way, you'll be transferring all your assets into heaven. And then, after that, come follow me."

Q. What did he say to that?

A. He walked away extremely sad. He was a very wealthy young man. But what good is all the wealth of the world if a man loses his own soul? How much money would someone take in exchange for his soul?

Q. Is this a new idea that you're preaching—that God intends for people who are well off to share the wealth?

A. *(Shaking his head.)* Let me tell you another story.

Q. All right.

A. There was a rich man who dressed himself in the most expensive clothes he could buy and who dined like a king every day. Outside the gate to this rich man's estate lay a beggar named Lazarus, whose body was covered with running sores. Every day Lazarus begged for scraps and leftovers from the rich man's table while the neighbourhood dogs came over and licked his sores. Finally Lazarus died and was carried by angels to be with Abraham. Later the rich man died, too, and he was sent to hell. There, tortured and tormented, he could look far into the distance and see Abraham and Lazarus. In his misery the rich man cried out, "Father Abraham! Have mercy on me! Send Lazarus to me so he can dip his finger in water and touch my tongue with it. I'm burning up!" But Abraham told him, "Son, do you remember that while you were alive, you had every good thing and Lazarus had every bad thing? Well, now he's comfortable, and *you're* the one who's in misery. That's the way it is. Besides that, there's an enormous chasm that separates us. Lazarus can't go where you are, and you can't come where we are." Then the rich man said, "Please, then, send somebody to my father's house to warn my brothers. I have five brothers. Send somebody to tell them where I am and what it's like so that they won't end up here, too." Abraham said, "Your brothers have Moses and the prophets to warn them. They can read those warnings in the Scripture." "No, father Abraham," the rich man answered, "they won't do that. But if somebody went to them from the dead, they would repent." "I don't think so," Abraham told him. "If they won't pay attention to Moses and the prophets, they won't be persuaded even if someone rises from the grave to tell them."

Q. Well, do you have any good news for rich folks? Is there any hope for them?

A. *(Another smile.)* Of course. I was passing through Jericho one day—I had just entered the city and was making my way through town—and I came to a place where there were some trees, some sycamores, along the side of the street. When I looked up, I saw a man up in one of the trees.

Q. What was he doing up there?

A. He was kind of short and couldn't see over the people who were crowding the edge of the street. Because he wanted to get a look at me, he had climbed up one of those trees to get a clear view.

Q. OK.

A. His name was Zaccheus, and he was one of the tax collectors in that district. In fact, he was the chief tax collector, appointed by the Roman administration. He was a Jew—a very rich Jew. When I saw him up there, I stopped and told him, "Come down out of that tree, Zaccheus. Hurry up. You're going to take me home to dinner today."

Q. That must have surprised him.

A. He came down as fast as he could and was all smiles, greeting me and welcoming me to the city and to his house. Of course there had to be a few soreheads in the crowd who criticized me for going home with a tax collector. But I went anyway. As I've told Pharisees and others before, it's the sick who need a physician, not the healthy. After Zaccheus and I had eaten and had had a chance to talk, he stood up and said to me, "Lord, from now on I'm giving half my wealth to the poor, and if I've cheated anybody, I'll pay him back four times whatever it was he paid to me."

Q. How about that?

A. "Surely salvation has come to this house today," I told him. "Zaccheus, a son of Abraham, is just the sort of person the Son of Man has come to seek and to save."

Giving and Receiving

Q. You've already said that tithing is important. But you've also suggested that giving a tenth in some cases may not be enough, as in the case of the rich young man who asked you what he had to do to gain eternal life. I wonder if you would clarify that matter of giving. Is a tenth sufficient to fulfill a person's obligation to give?

A. I was sitting near the collection boxes in the temple one day, and I was just quietly watching as people put money into those collection boxes. Some well-off people came by and dropped in large amounts. Then this woman, an obviously poor widow, came over and emptied her purse. She gave everything that was in her purse.

Q. OK.

A. It was two coins. That was all she had. Two coins. And she gave it all. *(A pause.)* I called my students over and told them, "This poor widow has given more than all those rich people put together. They gave what they could easily afford. She gave it all."

Q. Was that generous or foolish of her?

A. Here's the principle. Give, and it will be given to you—heaped up, pressed down, shaken up, compressed, stacked high, and running over. Whatever measure you use to give—a tenth, a half, the whole thing—that's the same measure that will be used to give back to you.

Anxiety and Money Worries

Q. But don't we have to be concerned about looking after ourselves? If I gave away my money, how would I feed myself? How would I pay my bills? How would I take care of my family? And what would happen when I got old? Would I then become dependent on others?

A. *(Nodding.)* Don't be anxious about tomorrow. Don't be forever worrying about what you're going to eat, what you're going to drink, what you're going to wear. Life is more than food, and the body is more than clothes. Look at the birds up there in the air. They don't plant, they don't harvest, and they don't store stuff in barns. Yet your heavenly Father feeds them. Believe me, you mean a lot more to him than those birds do. And why be so bothered about what you're going to wear? Take a look at the lilies growing in the field. They don't spend their hours spinning and weaving. But even King Solomon, in all his finery, never managed to look as good as those lilies do. So if God can dress up a field with wildflowers and blooming plants that blossom for a while and then are mowed down and burned up, isn't it reasonable to believe that he will provide you with something to wear? As for worrying about your body, why waste your time? Will all your worrying make you even an inch taller? The point is, you shouldn't be fretting and stewing about such things. You shouldn't be wringing your hands and saying, "What are we going to eat? What are we going to drink? What am I going to wear?" People who have little or no knowledge of God anguish over such things. They make eating and drinking a really big deal. Trust me on this: Your heavenly Father knows full well that you need the basics of life. What you should be concerned about is the Kingdom of God. You should make it your number one consideration. After all, a person doesn't live by bread alone. He lives by God's will for his life. A person should bend every effort to live up to God's high expectations. When he or she does, everything else will fall into place.

Q. You certainly seem to be living up to that idea. You don't actually have a home or property, do you?

A. Foxes have holes to live in, and birds have nests, but I don't even own a place where I can lay my head and rest. *(A pause.)* And everyone who has left home, land, and family to follow me will one day be rewarded a hundred times over for whatever was left behind. And he or she will inherit everlasting life.

Q. Well, that does help put things in perspective.

A. What I'm saying is, don't be overly concerned about the future. I think you'll find that there's plenty enough to worry about today; there's no need to take on tomorrow's worries before tomorrow even gets here.

Marriage and Divorce

Q. I'd like you to hear your views on marriage and divorce. What do you think about divorce?

A. Several Pharisees came to me one day and asked me about the same subject. They had their question all ready for me. "Is it legal," they said, "for a man to divorce his wife for whatever reason?" I asked them, "What did Moses tell you?" They said, "Moses said it was all right. He said a man could divorce his wife by writing out a notice of divorce." I told them, "Moses allowed divorce only because he was fed up and frustrated by your attitude. He gave up and let you do what you were determined to do. But if you've read your Scripture, you know that in the very beginning God created humans as male and female. 'For this reason a man shall leave his father and mother,' the Scripture says, 'and be joined to his wife, and the two shall become one flesh.' The two of them shall become one," I told them. "And what God joins together, man should not separate."

Q. What happens if a man divorces his wife anyway?

A. If a man divorces his wife and then marries someone else, he is guilty of adultery. If a woman divorces her husband and remarries, she is guilty of adultery. Anyone who marries a divorced woman is guilty of adultery.

Q. Not much leeway there, is there?

A. After my students heard me tell those Pharisees that, they double-checked with me to make sure I had said what they thought they heard me say. I repeated it for them. One of them then commented, "If that's the way it is, it doesn't seem like it's a good idea to ever get married."

Q. And what did you say to that?

A. I told them, as I now tell you, "What I'm saying is not for everybody. It's only for those to whom God directs the message. Some people are born without the ability to have sexual relations. Some have the inability forced on them by others. They're turned into eunuchs. And some forgo sex and marriage, and in effect become eunuchs, by their own choosing. They do so in order to serve the Kingdom of Heaven. Whoever can accept that, let him or her accept it."

Children

Q. I feel sure, though, that you don't want to give the impression that you're against marriage and family.

A. When I was with a large group one day, some parents came to me and brought their little ones, asking me to lay hands on them and bless them and pray for them. There were quite a few of them. My students thought all of this was an annoyance to me, so they started scolding the parents, telling them to stop forcing their children on me. When I saw what my students were doing, I got a little upset with them. "Let those children come on over to me!" I told them. "Don't keep them away! The Kingdom of God is made up of people like these little children. Let me tell you something as earnestly as I know how," I said. "Unless a person receives the Kingdom of God with wholehearted belief as these little children do, he or she will never enter it."

Q. So you went right on with the children?

A. I held them in my arms and put my hands on them and gave them my blessing.

Q. It must have been a heartwarming sight—especially for the parents.

A. *(A smile.)*

Q. I'm getting the feeling that you actually love little kids—not just tolerate them, but love them.

A. My students were having a big discussion one day, and they came to me with a question. I guess I was supposed to settle the matter they had been discussing. "Who is going to be the greatest in the Kingdom of Heaven?" they asked me.

There was a young boy standing nearby, and I called him over to me and had him face my students and the others who were there. "You see this little one? I'm going to tell you something. Unless you change your ways and become like this little child, you're not even going to make it into the Kingdom of Heaven. But if you humble yourself and take on the attitude of a sweet, accepting, innocent child, then you qualify to be called the greatest in the Kingdom of Heaven."

Q. OK.

A. If people take in a little child like that for my sake, they are, in effect, taking me in. But if someone becomes an impediment to the faith of a little child who believes in me, that person would be better off if a millstone were hung around his neck and he was thrown into the deepest part of the ocean and drowned.

Q. You're saying that there's a price to pay for causing someone to lose faith.

A. *(Wiping his forehead with the back of his hand.)* It's terrible that there is so much evil in the world. Even so, the person who gives in to evil is going to be held accountable.

The Kingdom of Heaven

Q. You keep mentioning the Kingdom of Heaven and the Kingdom of God. I wish you'd explain what you mean when you use those terms.

A. Several Pharisees asked me once when the Kingdom of God would come, and I had to tell them that the Kingdom is not going to come with some sort of signs that you'll be able to observe and tell that it's arrived. You won't be able to say, "Look, here it is! Look, there it is!" That's not the kind of kingdom it is. The Kingdom of God is within you.

Q. It's personal.

A. Let me illustrate. The Kingdom of Heaven is like the situation that arose with ten bridesmaids who were supposed to be in a wedding party. They all took their oil lamps and went out into the evening to meet the bridegroom. Five of them were smart, and five of them were foolish. The foolish ones took their lamps but no extra oil. The smart ones took not only their lamps but also an extra supply of oil. When the bridegroom took more time than the bridesmaids expected, they all fell asleep and didn't wake up until midnight, when someone started shouting, "The bridegroom's coming! Get up and go greet him!" The bridesmaids jumped up and started turning up their lamps. That was when the five foolish ones realized they were out of fuel. "Give us some of your oil!" they demanded of the smart ones. "Our lamps have gone out!" The smart ones told them, "We can't do it. We wouldn't have enough for our own lamps. Go to the store and get some." So off they went to get more. While they were gone, the bridegroom finally arrived, and the five smart bridesmaids were able to accompany him into the house where the wedding banquet was being held. Once everyone was inside, the doors were shut and locked. After a while, the five foolish bridesmaids came back to the house with their new oil and found they were locked out. They started shouting, "Sir, open the door for us!" But the lord of the house refused. "I don't know who you are," he told them.

Q. You're saying the Kingdom of Heaven is something that, if people are wise, they will make sure they are prepared for. Is that right?

A. The Kingdom of Heaven is like the situation that occurred when a man was about to leave on a long trip. He called in his servants and turned over his property to them to take care of while he was gone. He gave ten thousand dollars to one of them, five thousand to another, and one thousand to the other one. Then he left town. The servant who had been entrusted with the ten thousand took it, invested it, and earned an additional ten thousand. The one who had been given the five thousand used it to earn another five thousand. The servant who had been given one thousand dollars took the money, went out in the field, dug a hole, and hid the money in the hole. After being gone a long time, the boss came back from his trip and called in his servants to have them account for the money he had entrusted to them. The servant who had been given the ten thousand dollars brought it and the money he had earned with it, and he told the boss, "Here's what I've done. I've doubled your money." The boss was delighted. "You've done well. You're a good and faithful servant. And because you've done so well with the relatively small amount I gave you, I'm going to give you a promotion and give you responsibility for much more. Consider yourself one of my best workers." The servant who had been given five thousand dollars also came and reported. "Sir, I took your five thousand dollars and worked it up to ten thousand. Here it is." "Well done," the boss told him. "You've shown yourself to be a good and faithful worker, and I'm going to promote you and give you more responsibility. You have my sincere gratitude." Then the third servant made his report to the boss. "Sir," he said, "I'm well aware that you're a hard man, taking every advantage you can, and I was afraid to take a chance and risk losing your money. So I buried it. And here it is back, the whole amount. One thousand dollars. I didn't lose a dollar of it." "What laziness! What stupidity!" the boss told him. "You know I'm a man who never lets an advantage slip past me. You know I make demands on people! And you just sat on the money! You could have at least put it in the bank and let it draw interest!" Then he took the thousand from his servant and turned it over to the servant who had been given the ten thousand. "The man who has been faithful with what I have given him will get a lot more," the boss told his workers, "but the man who was not faithful with what I gave him will lose what little he does have. Now, take this unproductive servant and throw him out into the darkness and let him moan and groan."

Q. I think your meaning is becoming clearer to me. But I'm not sure.

A. It's like this. A vineyard owner needed workers to harvest his grapes, and he went out early in the morning and hired a crew of workers, promising to pay each one twenty dollars. About nine o'clock that same morning, he went back into town, saw some men standing around, and recruited them to pick grapes, too. "I'll pay you a fair wage at the end of the day," he told them. About noon and again at three in the afternoon he went back into town again and hired more workers, telling them, too, that he would pay them a fair wage at the end of the day. Around five o'clock that afternoon he was in town again and saw more men with nothing to do, and he asked them, "Why are you just standing around doing nothing?" They told him, "Because nobody's offered us a job." "Well, you can work for me," he said. "Go to my vineyard, and get busy. I'll pay you a fair amount at the end of the day." So when the sun had gone down, the vineyard owner had everybody line up for his pay. He told his cashier to give the last men hired their pay first, and the men who had been hired first would be paid last. When the workers who had been hired late in the day got their money, they were pleased to see that the owner paid them twenty dollars. The ones who had been hired early in the day then figured they'd get more than twenty, since they had worked longer. But they got twenty dollars, too. Then they started complaining to the vineyard owner. "These men here worked just one hour, and you paid them the same thing you gave us, after we'd worked and sweated in the sun all day." "Wait a minute," the owner told them. "I haven't done you any wrong, my friend. Didn't you agree to do a full day's work for twenty dollars? Here it is, then. Take it, and be on your way. If I want to pay everybody the same, I'll do it. After all, it's my money. Can't I spend it whatever way I want to? You're going to be angry with me because I'm generous?" Those who are last are going to be first, and those who are first will be last.

Q. Could you give me one more little example? I'm struggling.

A. *(A smile.)* The Kingdom of God is like a mustard seed, a tiny little seed that a man took and planted in his yard. This seed started growing and eventually became a huge tree with branches where birds could build their nests. The Kingdom of God is also like yeast that a woman mixed into three cups of flour so that the whole batch of bread dough was fermented and would rise when it was baked. It's also like the situation where a farmer scatters seed on the ground, then goes about his business. All the while the seeds sprout and grow, but the farmer has no idea exactly how the seeds grow. The soil produces from the seed a sprout, then a plant, then the grain on the plant. And when the grain is ripe, the farmer comes with his sickle to gather it in because harvesttime has arrived.

Q. OK.

A. Here's the way I think of it. The Kingdom of Heaven is like treasure hidden in a field. A man stumbles onto it, realizes what it is, then hides it again. With his heart pounding in excitement, he goes and sells everything he has to buy that field with the treasure in it.

Q. Yes, I see.

A. It's like a jewel merchant looking for pearls, and when he finds the one better than all the rest, he sells what he has and buys that one.

What His Followers Can Expect

Q. Maybe we're ready to move on to something else. I'd like to have you tell me about the training program that you have for your students.

A. I've given them instruction, spent many hours with them. And I've sent them out to practice what they've learned so they'll get experience.

Q. Experience at healing?

A. Yes, among other things.

Q. They have the same power to heal that you do?

A. *(Nodding.)* I've enabled them to drive out evil spirits and to heal the sick—heal every kind of disease, ailment, and disability that they might encounter.

Q. Have they already done that? Gone out and tried their hand at healing?

A. Yes.

Q. Where did they go?

A. Around Galilee mostly. I told them not to go to heathen communities and not to go into any towns in Samaria. I told them to go to the lost sheep of Israel.

Q. What were they to do besides heal?

A. As they went from place to place, they were to announce to people that the Kingdom of Heaven is coming. Along with delivering that message, they were to heal the sick, raise the dead, cure lepers, and cast out demons.

Q. Were they to get paid for what they did, charge fees as doctors do?

A. Absolutely not. "Give in the same way you have received," I told them. "Without charge."

Q. How would they support themselves if they were gone for some lengthy period? Would they take enough money with them to live on?

A. No. I told them not to take money with them. No money, no extra clothes, no spare sandals, no baggage of any kind, not even a walking stick.

Q. So how were they to get along?

A. Their main needs were food and shelter. Those whom they helped, I told them, would help them in return. They would provide for their needs.

Q. Did it work out that way?

A. *(A grin and a shrug.)* Usually. "When you go into a town," I told them, "try to find someone who is respected there and will take you in. Stay with that person or that family until you're ready to move on to the next town or community. When you enter the house of your host," I told them, "pronounce your blessing upon it. If the family makes you feel welcome there, your blessing will be deserved. If they don't prove hospitable, however, revoke your blessing and leave. If you come across a home or a community where it's obvious you're not welcome, where people won't even listen to what you have to say, leave and don't have anything more to do with them. Shake your sandals when you leave, and rid yourself of the dirt of that place."

Q. And that would be the end of all dealings with that town?

A. As far as my students are concerned, yes. But not so far as the community is concerned. As I told the twelve, come Judgment Day, God's punishment for that disrespectful, unreceptive, inhospitable community will make his judgment on the cities of Sodom and Gomorrah seem lenient.

Q. Did you actually expect your students to encounter bad treatment, maybe even hostility?

A. *(Nodding.)* Oh yes. Yes indeed. I warned them of it. I told them to expect it. "I'm sending you like sheep out where the wolves roam," I said. "Be aware of the dangers. Watch your step. Be as cautious as snakes but as gentle as doves. You're going to run into trouble sooner or later," I told them. "For the good that you're doing you'll be arrested and dragged into court. They'll flog you in their synagogues. Because of me, they'll force you to stand trial before governors and kings even. You'll have to stand up and say things about me."

Q. Good things or bad?

A. *(Another nod.)* Ah, that's the point. "When you're hauled into court," I told them, "and you're ordered to testify in front of high officials, see it as an opportunity to witness for me, to give your testimony to those officials and to the world."

Q. If you knew things like that were going to happen to them, was there some speech, some sermon that you prepared them to deliver at the appropriate time?

A. No. I told them, "When they arrest you, don't worry about what you're going to say at your hearing or your trial. At that time, when you're facing your antagonists, when the authorities are waiting to hear your testimony, the Spirit of your Father will speak through you. The words that you hear coming out of your mouth will be issuing not from your own mind but from the mind of your Father."

Q. It sounds as if being one of your followers might sometimes be hazardous to one's health.

A. *(A somber expression on his face.)* I tell my friends that they should not fear those who can kill the body but that's all they can do. The one to fear is the one who not only has the power of life and death but also has the power to cast into hell. He is the one to fear.

Q. You give your followers fair warning.

A. Yes. Those who believe in me are going to find that their relationships with their friends and their families have been disrupted by their faith in me. People are going to turn against them. A brother will betray his brother and turn him in to be executed for heresy or blasphemy. Fathers will turn in their children. Children will betray their parents and have them put to death. If you're my follower, everyone is going to hate you, because of me.

Q. Everyone?

A. *(A shrug.)* I think you know what I mean.

Q. Well, it's a bleak outlook that you paint for your followers.

A. It's realistic. The good news is that those who persevere, those who stick with me to the end, will be saved; they will make it home safe and sound.

Q. Being one of your followers, then, is something like an endurance test.

A. That's one way of looking at it. People shouldn't think that I've come to bring peace to the world. I haven't. What I'm bringing is a sword.

Q. I'm not sure I understand that.

A. I've come to set a man at odds with his father. I've come to set a daughter against her mother. A daughter-in-law against her mother-in-law. People who are my followers will find that their worst enemies are members of their own families.

Q. That's pretty rough stuff.

A. People who care more about their father or mother than they do about me, who are influenced more by their parents than by me, are not worthy of me. And the same can be said about parents who care more about their sons or daughters than about me. People who refuse to take up their cross and follow me are not worthy of me.

Q. Is it complete self-denial you're asking of your followers?

A. The person who is intent on holding on to his or her life will lose it. But the person who gives up his life for my sake will gain it. Do you understand that?

Q. I . . . think so.

A. No one can be my disciple unless he is willing to carry his cross and follow behind me. *(A pause.)* People need to realize what they're getting into before they take an important step. It's like a man who wants to build a building. Before he begins construction, he sits down and figures out how much it's going to cost and decides whether he's got enough financing to complete the construction. Otherwise, he's likely to lay the foundation and start putting up the walls and then suddenly realize he's run out of money. The building is left standing there, half finished. And everybody who goes by and sees it laughs and thinks that was a stupid thing to do. "See what this man has done?" people will say. "He had a big idea for this building, but he wasn't smart enough to figure out how to finance it." Or to give another example, when a king is planning to lead his army into battle, doesn't he first meet with his advisers and try to determine how his army of ten thousand is going to be able to take on an army of twenty thousand? If he and his advisers can't see how it can be done, they'll have to dispatch an envoy to the other king and cut a deal that will avoid war.

Q. Would you say that being a follower of yours is a difficult life?

A. I say to people, "Come to me, all of you who feel weighed down and are struggling with your load in life. I'll give you relief. Put on my yoke, and let me guide you. You'll learn that I am gentle and humble, and with me you'll find rest for your souls. My yoke is easily worn, and my burden is light."

Q. I would think that a lot of people would respond to that invitation.

A. Entrance to the Kingdom is through the narrow gate. The path that leads to destruction is wide and smoothly paved. Its entrance gate is wide, and there are a great many who pass through it. But strait is the gate and narrow the way that leads to life, and there are few who find their way.

Leadership and Ministry

Q. "Gentle and humble," the two qualities you mentioned, don't seem to be in keeping with the image that people generally have of the expected messiah. I guess you're operating under a different set of standards.

A. People in authority who have no knowledge of God like to lord it over their subordinates and those of lower status. But that's not the way it's to be among my followers. Whoever wants to be a leader must become a servant to the others. Whoever wants to be their chief must become their slave. The would-be leader needs to notice that the Son of Man didn't come to be ministered to. He came to minister. He didn't come to have people serve him. He came to serve people. And to give his life as a ransom for many of them.

Love and Obedience

Q. From what I've seen and heard, you've attracted quite a following. People hold you not just in awe but in great affection. How should people show their affection for you?

A. If people really love me, they'll follow my instructions. They will do as I've taught them. The person who *doesn't* do as I've instructed doesn't love me. It's that simple. If you love me, obey me. Whoever loves me will be loved by my Father. And I'll love those people, too, and let them know it. My Father and I will come to them and remain with them. Here's the way people can show the world that they are my followers—love one another. Servants are not greater than their master. What I do, I expect my followers to do. In the same way I have loved them, they are to love one another.

Q. Speaking of showing love for you, I get the impression from Martha that she is someone who has a great affection for you. Is she an old friend?

A. *(A smile.)* I have a story about Martha.

Q. I'd like to hear it.

A. It goes back to when I first met Martha and her sister, Mary, and their brother, Lazarus. I had come to Bethany with the twelve, and we needed a place to stay. Martha invited us to stay at her house, here. *(Waving his hand.)* So we accepted her invitation, and she gave us food and lodging. While we were eating, I was talking, and Mary was sitting there listening to me. Martha, on the other hand, was busy serving everybody. Single-handedly, she was serving us all. After a while, she got upset that Mary was just sitting there while she—Martha—was doing all the work. So finally she came to me and told me, "Lord, don't you care that my sister has left me to do all the work by myself? Tell her to come help me."

Q. Not exactly shy or overawed, was she?

A. *(A smile.)* I said, "Martha, Martha. You're letting too many things worry you. There's only one really important thing in life to be concerned about, and Mary has chosen that thing as her concern. I'm not going to keep her from it."

Q. So Mary chose the right thing—spending time with you, learning about your ideas.

A. Yes.

Q. You do see these people, your followers, as your friends, don't you? I mean, they're a lot closer to you than just adherents or fans, aren't they?

A. I love them. I don't call the twelve my "servants." I call them "friends." Servants don't know what their master is doing. They're not kept informed. But I share with my friends what my Father is telling me to do. Everything that I've heard from my Father I've told them. Especially have I told them to love one another.

Israel's Lost Opportunity

Q. Official Israel—the Pharisees and other religious leaders anyway—have pretty much rejected you. Is it possible that their reaction to you might change your mission?

A. I'll answer that with a couple of stories. *(A pause.)* A landowner planted a large vineyard on his land and then had a hedge planted around the vineyard. He also installed a winepress and had a tower built so the vineyard could be guarded from trespassers. Then he leased out the vineyard to some tenant farmers, and he went off to another country. When grape harvest came, the landowner sent several servants to collect his share of the crop. The tenant farmers, however, beat up one of the servants, murdered another one, and stoned another one. The landowner then sent another delegation of servants, a larger group this time. The tenants did the same to them as to the earlier group. After that, the landowner decided to send his son to deal with the tenants. "They'll show respect for my son," he reasoned. But when the tenants saw the son coming, they got together and said, "This is the owner's heir. Let's kill him, and then the vineyard will become ours!" So they captured him, forced him out of the vineyard, and then murdered him. *(A pause.)* Now when the landowner himself comes to the vineyard, what do you think he's going to do to those tenants?

Q. I'd expect him to wipe them out and find himself a new set of tenants.

A. That's the answer some priests and Pharisees gave me when I asked them the same question. It's the correct answer. "The Kingdom of God is going to be taken away from you," I told those Pharisees and priests, "and it's going to be given to a nation that produces fruit for the Kingdom."

Q. Did they realize what you meant?

A. *(A nod.)* They wanted to arrest me but were afraid of what the crowd would do to them. *(Another pause.)* Here's another story. There was a king who was planning a wedding for his son. It was to be a big, elaborate celebration with many guests. When the time came, he sent out his servants to escort the invited guests to the banquet. But they refused to come. Then the king sent out other servants to tell the invited guests: "The food and everything else are prepared and ready for you. It's going to be a huge feast. We urge you to come." But the invited guests again refused to come. They made light of the banquet and went off and did other things, one returning to his farm, another to his store. Still other invited guests seized the king's servants, beat them up, and killed them. When the king heard about this response, he ordered out his army to destroy the murderers and burn their city to the ground. Then to his servants the king said, "We're still going to have a wedding. The people I invited didn't deserve to be invited. So go out on the road and invite everybody you can find." They did. They came back with all kinds of people, good and bad alike, and filled the banquet hall with them. When the king came into the hall to get a look at those who had come, he saw a man who hadn't bothered to dress for the occasion. He asked the man, "Friend, why did you show up without having dressed yourself appropriately for the banquet?" The man had no answer. The king told his servants, "Tie him up and throw him out into the darkness where all that weeping and regretting are going on. For although many are called, few are chosen."

Judgment Day

Q. How will you decide who will be chosen, who will have a place in the Kingdom of Heaven?

A. This is what the Kingdom of Heaven is like. It's like a farmer who planted good wheat seed in his field, and then one night, while everyone was asleep, one of his enemies came and scattered weed seeds all over the field. When the wheat seeds sprouted, the weeds came up, too. The farmer's workers came and told him what was happening. "Wasn't that good seed that we planted?" they asked him. "Why are there weeds mixed in with the wheat shoots?" "Somebody who hates me has done this to me," the farmer said. "Do you want us to go pull up the weeds?" the workers asked him. "No," the farmer told them, "I'm afraid some of the wheat plants will get pulled up along with the weeds. Let the wheat and weeds grow up side by side until harvesttime. Then the reaping crew can cut the weeds first and gather them up in bundles and burn them. After that, they can harvest the wheat and put it in my barn."

Q. The harvest is the day of judgment. Right?

A. *(A nod.)* I am the farmer who sows the good seed. The field is the world. The good seed are the people of the Kingdom, and the weeds are the people who belong to Satan. The enemy who sowed the weeds is Satan. The harvest is the end of the world, and the reapers are angels. Just as the weeds in the story are gathered and burned, it will be the same way at the end of the world. I will send my angels, and they will cull out everyone who doesn't belong in the Kingdom of Heaven.

They'll remove all the causes of sin and evil and the evildoers as well. They'll throw them into a furnace and burn them up. There's going to be a lot of weeping and gnashing of teeth when that happens. Then the good people—those who have chosen to live up to God's expectations—are going to have their day. They're going to shine out like the sun in the King-dom of their Father.

Q. A graphic picture, I'd say.

A. Or to use another illustration, the day of judgment is like a net that fishermen cast out into the water, and the net cap-tured all kinds of fish. When the net was full, the fishermen hauled it up onto shore and sat down and started sorting through the fish. The good ones they kept and put in baskets. The bad ones—the rough, inedible ones—they threw away. *(A pause.)* That's how it's going to be at the end of the world. The angels will come and sort out the good and the bad.

Q. I suppose that will come as a big surprise to many people.

A. No one should be surprised, but the time is coming when even the dead in their graves will hear the voice of the Son of Man, and they will come forth—those who have done good will rise to the resurrection of life, and those who have done evil will rise to the resurrection of damnation. Anyone who hears what I'm saying and believes on him who sent me will receive everlasting life and will not face the judgment. Those who believe have already passed from death into life.

Q. A sobering thought.

A. When the Son of Man returns like a king in glory, escorted by all the holy angels, he will take his place on the throne of his glory, and before him will be assembled all the nations of the earth. He will separate the people, one from the other, just as a shepherd separates his sheep from the goats. He will place the sheep at his right hand and the goats at his left. Then the king will say to those at his right hand, "Come, you who are blessed by my Father. Inherit the kingdom that has been prepared for you since the beginning of the world. When I was hungry, you fed me. When I was thirsty, you gave me something to drink. When I was a stranger, you took me in. I was naked, and you clothed me. I was sick, and you visited me. I was in prison, and you came to see me." Then the righteous people will ask, "Lord, when was it that we saw you hungry and fed you, or thirsty and gave you something to drink? When did we see you as a stranger and take you in, or naked and give you clothes? When did we see you sick or in prison and come to visit you?" And the king will give them this answer: "I tell you truly, when you did those things for the very least of any of these who are my brothers, you did them for me." Then the king will turn to those at his left hand and tell them, "Get out of my presence, you accursed creatures! Go into the eternal fire that's been prepared for the devil and his angels! I was hungry, and you gave me nothing to eat. I was thirsty, and you didn't give me anything to drink. I was a stranger, and you didn't take me in. I was naked, and you gave me nothing to wear. I was sick and I was in prison, and you didn't come to visit me." Then they'll say, "But, Lord, when did we see you hungry or thirsty or a stranger or sick or in prison and didn't do something for you?" At that point, the king will tell them, "I'm telling you the truth, when you didn't do those things for one of the most humble of these, you didn't do it for me." And from there they will go away into eternal punishment. But the righteous will enter into eternal life.

Resurrection

Q. I understand that the resurrection is a controversial subject. One group, the Sadducees, insists that there's no such thing. But many Pharisees and others believe there is a resurrection. What do you say about it?

A. Some Sadducees have asked me about that, too. They say there is no resurrection after death. I asked them if they have ever read the words in Scripture where God speaks and says, "I *am* the God of Abraham and the God of Isaac and the God of Jacob." God is the God not of the dead but of the living.

Q. You mean if Abraham, Isaac, and Jacob were dead and not resurrected, God would have identified himself in the past tense. He would have said, "I *was* the God of Abraham."

A. *(A nod.)* In truth I tell you that I am the resurrection and I am life. The power to give life is part of me. The people who believe in me, even though they die, will live again. And the people who live and believe in me will never die.

Heaven

Q. In heaven, after their resurrection, do people resume the lives they lived on earth?

A. Several Sadducees had a similar question for me not long ago. They came up with a hypothetical situation and then asked me to resolve it.

Q. What was it?

A. They said, "Teacher, Moses wrote for us that if a man's brother has a wife but no children and he dies, the surviving brother should marry the widow and have children by her so that the dead brother will have heirs. Well, there was this family of seven brothers, and the oldest one married and then died without children. The second oldest married the widow, had no children, and died. The third oldest then married the woman, and he also died childless. It happened to one after the other, so that all seven brothers married the woman, and none of them had children. Then the woman herself died. Now then, at the time for resurrection, whose wife will she be?"

Q. An interesting question. What did you tell them?

A. I told them that men and women in this world marry, but those who are deemed worthy to enter heaven and to be given resurrection do not marry. They never die again. They are like angels. They are the children of God, having been resurrected to a new kind of life.

Q. Will you be in heaven, too?

A. There are a great many suites in my Father's palace. I'm going to go prepare a place there for every one of my followers. When everything is ready, I'm coming back to get them and take them there, so that they're going to be where I am.

Q. And the people you don't come to get won't get there?

A. I am the way to get there. I'm the way to truth and to life. No one will come to the Father except through me. *(A pause.)* My sheep know my voice, and I know them. They follow me, and I give them eternal life. They'll never know death, and they'll never be taken away from me. My Father is the one who has given them to me, and he has greater power than anyone, than everyone all together. No one will ever be able to pry them from my Father's hand.

The End of the World

Q. I think the end of the world is a subject that fascinates a lot of people. People want to know what's going to happen and when it's going to happen and how they can tell that it's about to happen. I wish you would share your insights about the end.

A. Be careful that you aren't fooled. Many people will be coming and saying, "I am the Christ!" And they're going to deceive a lot of people. And you'll hear of wars and rumors of wars. But don't be worried. Those things will have to take place. But they don't mean the end. A nation will go to war against another nation. A kingdom will wage war against another kingdom. And there will be famines and epidemics and earthquakes in various places. Those occurrences will be like the pains that precede childbirth.

Q. And then what?

A. Then my followers will be arrested and tortured and killed. In every land they'll be hated because they have taken on my name, because they're Christians. And many of them will recant their faith and will betray fellow Christians and will hate them. Many false prophets will appear and will mislead a lot of people. Sin and evil will be so widespread that they will have a chilling effect on many a good and loving person.

Q. That's a terrifying forecast.

A. But the person who hangs on until the end, that person will be saved. And the good news of the Kingdom will be proclaimed all over the world, so that everyone everywhere can hear it. After that, the end will come.

Q. The end—what will it be like?

A. When they see the abominable defilement of the holy place, about which the prophet Daniel spoke, everybody in Judea should flee to the mountains. People who are outside shouldn't take time to go inside the house and get anything. Those who are out working in the field shouldn't go home for their good clothes. And pity the poor woman who is pregnant! And the ones who still have a baby at their breast! People should pray that their flight to refuge won't come in the winter or on a Sabbath. It will be a time of such intense horror! It will be like nothing the world has ever seen before or ever will again. It will be so terrible that if it were to continue, no one would survive.

Q. How will it be stopped?

A. For the sake of his chosen people, God will stop it. If at that time someone says to you, "Look, here is the Christ!" or, "There he is!" don't believe it. There will be a great many false Christs and false prophets, and they'll perform all sorts of tricks and wonders. The things that they'll do will be so persuasive that if it were possible for God's people to be taken in by them, they would. Be forewarned. If people say, "Christ is in the wilderness!" don't go. If they say, "He's in the back room!" don't believe it. Just as lightning that flashes across the eastern sky is seen in the west, so shall the coming of the Son of Man be. Just as the gathering of the vultures indicates where the carcass lies, so do these signs indicate that the end of the world is coming soon.

Q. What else will happen?

A. After the ordeal of those days, the sun will go dark, the moon will give no light, and stars will appear to fall from the sky. The very forces of nature will be shaken. Then the sign of the Son of Man will appear in the sky. And then tears will come to the eyes of people of every nation, every ethnic group, as they see the Son of Man, with great power and glory, coming in the clouds of the sky. He will dispatch his angels with a mighty trumpet call, and the angels will gather together God's chosen people from the four corners of the earth and from one end of heaven to the other.

Q. What a scene.

A. There's a lesson to be learned from the fig tree. When its branches begin to bud and it starts to put out leaves, you know that summer is well on its way. So when you see the things that I've described begin to happen, you can be sure that the time is near. It's practically at your front door. *(A pause.)* This generation is not going to pass away before these things happen. Heaven and earth may pass away, but not my words.

Q. But you won't say how far in the future those things will occur.

A. I don't know the day and hour. The angels in heaven don't know either. Only my Father knows. *(A pause.)* Just as it was in Noah's time, when no one knew exactly when the flood would come, that's the way it is with the coming of the Son of Man at the end. In the days before the flood, people were eating and drinking, marrying and arranging marriages, right up to the day that Noah entered the ark. They didn't know the flood was coming until it actually hit them and swept them all away. That's the way it's going to be when the Son of Man returns. Two men will be working together in the field, and one of them will be taken, and the other one will be left. Two women will be together grinding at the mill, and one will be taken, and the other one left. So you need to be on your guard because you don't know the time when your Lord will come.

Q. It's going to come as a surprise.

A. It's like a homeowner who had his house burglarized. If he had known when the thieves would come and break into his house, he'd have stayed awake and been ready for them and wouldn't have let them break in. Or it's like a man who leaves on a long trip, and before he goes, he turns the tasks of his estate over to his servants, giving each one certain responsibilities. Then he tells his gatekeeper to watch for his return. "Keep your eyes open," he says, "for you don't know when I'll show up—whether in the evening, at midnight, at dawn, or midmorning. Make sure I don't find you sleeping. And what I'm telling the gatekeeper," he tells his other servants, "I say to all of you. Keep watching!" When he does come, it will be a happy surprise for the ones who are watching for him. He'll have those servants sit down at his table. He'll do the serving himself, and they'll be treated as guests at a dinner. The point is, always be ready because the Son of Man will come when you don't expect him.

Obstacles to Faith

Q. What would you say are the biggest obstacles to believing in you? What is the main thing that keeps people from believing?

A. This evil and unfaithful generation wants to see a sign. They are people who require proof. They've got to have proof of what I'm saying before they will believe. But, I tell you, the only proof that they're going to get is the sign of the prophet Jonah.

Q. Which was?

A. Jonah spent three days and three nights in the belly of the whale. And the Son of Man will spend three days and three nights in the heart of the earth. On Judgment Day the people of Nineveh will rise and condemn this generation. When Jonah preached in Nineveh, the people turned away from their wicked ways and turned to God. But now someone greater than Jonah is preaching to this people, and they refuse to believe him. The queen of Sheba will rise at the Judgment and also condemn this people. She traveled a great distance from her own country to seek the wisdom of King Solomon, and now someone greater than Solomon is here where Solomon was, and this generation refuses to listen to what he has to say. These wicked people are like a man who has a demon. The demon leaves the man and tries to find itself a better home. When it fails, it returns to the man and finds the man's heart clean but vacant. And so it calls seven other demons to join it, demons more satanic than itself, and they all move in to possess the man anew.

The result is that the man ends up being much worse off when the demon comes back than he was before the demon left him. That's the same situation that this evil generation will find itself in.

His Death and Resurrection

Q. You said you're going to spend three days and three nights in the heart of the earth. What do you mean by that?

A. The Son of Man will be betrayed and handed over to be crucified. The chief priests and the law experts will condemn me to death.

Q. Crucified?

A. *(A nod.)* When I am lifted up from the earth, I will draw everyone to me. *(A pause.)* In a little while I'll be gone, and my friends won't see me. But in another little while I'll be back. They'll see me again. I am going to the Father.

Q. I'm not sure I understand that exactly.

A. I'm going to be forced to go through a painful ordeal. I'll be rejected by the elders, by the chief priests, and by the law experts. I'll be turned over to the Romans, and I'll be mocked and scourged and spat upon. And then I'll be crucified. And after three days, I will rise again.

Q. Do your students know this?

A. I've told them plainly what is going to happen.

Q. Isn't there something they can do about it?

A. *(Shaking his head.)* Like them, you don't understand. You're thinking like humans, not like God. *(A pause.)* No one has greater love than the person who lays down his life for his friends, and my friends are those who do as I have instructed them. This is all happening in order to fulfill what the Scripture says: "They hated me for no reason."

Q. It seems like such a tragedy.

A. No one is taking my life from me. I am laying it down of my own free will. I have power to lay it down, and I have power to take it up again. I received this mission from my Father.

Q. It still seems a hard thing to accept.

A. *(Shaking his head again.)* Unless a kernel of wheat falls into the ground and dies, it remains alone. But if it dies, it produces many other kernels. *(A pause.)* People who want to be my followers must subordinate themselves and take up their cross and follow me. If saving your own life is your first consideration, you're going to end up losing it. But those who disregard their life for my sake and the sake of the Good News will find that their life has been saved.

Q. How did your students take it when you told them what was going to happen to you?

A. I told them it was to their advantage that I go away because if I didn't go away, the Divine Helper would not come to be with them. But if I leave, I will send him to them.

Q. What will this Divine Helper do?

A. He will make the world realize the difference between sin and goodness and will make it aware of the judgment that is to come.

Leaving Him

"Rabbi," I told him as I started to stand, "I want you to know that I'm truly grateful for this time with you. I thank you very much for sharing your time, your words, and yourself."

He stood, too, smiling and nodding his acknowledgment of my thanks. At that moment I had a strong feeling that I wanted to hug him, that I wanted to express something that I was feeling but didn't know how to say in words. He must have sensed what I was feeling because when I took a step toward him, he held out his arms. Then I held out mine, and we embraced. When I backed away, I said, "God willing, sir, I'll see you again." I was finding it hard to accept the thought that this was the end of my contact with him.

He smiled again. "I can see," he told me, "that you are not far from the Kingdom of Heaven."

"Thank you, Rabbi." Then I turned and with immense reluctance walked out of the room.

Scripture Reference Guide

CHILDREN (p. 67)

> Matthew 19:13-15
> Matthew 18:1-7

THE KINGDOM OF HEAVEN (p. 69)

> Luke 17:20-21
> Matthew 25:1-13
> Matthew 25:14-30
> Matthew 20:1-16
> Matthew 13:31-33
> Mark 4:26-29
> Matthew 13:44-46

WHAT HIS FOLLOWERS CAN EXPECT (p. 73)

> Matthew 10:5-20
> Matthew 10:28
> Matthew 10:21-22
> Matthew 10:34-39
> Luke 14:27-32
> Matthew 11:28-30
> Matthew 7:13-14

LEADERSHIP AND MINISTRY (p. 79)

> Matthew 20:25-28

LOVE AND OBEDIENCE (p. 81)

> John 14:15, 23-24
> Matthew 10:24-25
> John 15:12
> John 13:34-35
> Luke 10:38-42
> John 15:14-15
> John 15:12

ISRAEL'S LOST OPPORTUNITY (p. 83)

> Matthew 21:33-46
> Matthew 22:1-14